GOD BLESS HER!

QUEEN ELIZABETH
THE QUEEN MOTHER

ROBERT LACEY

CENTURY

LONDON MELBOURNE AUCKLAND JOHANNESBURG

for Scarlett, my daughter

PRIVATE CORRESPONDENCE REPRODUCED BY KIND PERMISSION
OF HER MAJESTY QUEEN ELIZABETH THE QUEEN MOTHER
QUOTATIONS FROM *PHOTOBIOGRAPHY* BY CECIL BEATON (1951) BY
KIND PERMISSION OF THE LITERARY EXECUTORS SIR CECIL BEATON ESTATE

FIRST PUBLISHED IN 1987 BY CENTURY HUTCHINSON LTD,
BROOKMOUNT HOUSE, 62–65 CHANDOS PLACE, COVENT GARDEN, LONDON WC2N 4NW

CENTURY HUTCHINSON AUSTRALIA PTY LTD, PO BOX 496
16–22 CHURCH STREET, HAWTHORN, VICTORIA 3122, AUSTRALIA

CENTURY HUTCHINSON NEW ZEALAND LIMITED,
PO BOX 40-086, GLENFIELD, AUCKLAND 10, NEW ZEALAND

CENTURY HUTCHINSON SOUTH AFRICA (PTY) LTD, PO BOX 337, BERGVLEI,
2012 SOUTH AFRICA

SET IN LINOTRON PERPETUA
PRINTED AND BOUND IN WEST GERMANY BY MOHNDRUCK GRAPHISCHE BETRIEBE GMBH
BRITISH LIBRARY CATALOGUING IN PUBLICATION DATA
LACEY, ROBERT
GOD BLESS HER!: HER MAJESTY QUEEN ELIZABETH
THE QUEEN MOTHER
1. ELIZABETH, *QUEEN, CONSORT OF GEORGE VI.
KING OF GREAT BRITAIN*   2. GREAT BRITAIN
———— QUEENS ———— BIOGRAPHY
I. TITLE
941.084'092'4   DA585.A2

ISBN 0 7126 1703 5

ART DIRECTION AND DESIGN BY BOB HOOK
PICTURE RESEARCH BY SARA DRIVER

*Cover, Queen Elizabeth photographed by Cecil Beaton in July
1939. Previous page, Queen Elizabeth photographed by Cecil
Beaton in 1948. Opposite, triptych of the Duchess of York painted
by Samuel Warburton, c. 1924.*

PICTURE CREDITS

Cover, frontispiece & pages 49, 50, 51, 54–55, 57, 66, 67, 76–77, 80–81, 82, 83 – Cecil Beaton reproduced by courtesy of
Eileen Hose; Contents page portrait by Samuel Warburton (c. 1924) – Private collection; Pages 24 (top), 32, 56 (bottom), 60
(top), 68, 69 (top), 74, 78, 79 – Popperfoto; 24 (bottom), 31, 34 (top), 75 (*Daily Mirror* front cover loaned by John Frost
Newspapers) – Syndication International; 25 Lady Bowes-Lyons by Mabel E. Hankey 1908, 29 Duchess of York by Philip de
Laszlo 1925, 33 Duchess of York by Savely Sorine 1923, 45 Queen Elizabeth by Sir Gerald Kelly c. 1938, 63 Queen Elizabeth
by Augustus John 1940, reproduced by Gracious Permission of Her Majesty the Queen; 44 (left) Queen Elizabeth – Sketch by
Sir Gerald Kelly c. 1938 – Windsor Castle, Royal Library – © Her Majesty the Queen; 26, 28 (bottom), 30, 36 (bottom), 43,
44 Queen Elizabeth by Sir Gerald Kelly c. 1938 (right), 73 Conversation Piece at the Royal Lodge, Windsor, by Sir James
Gunn 1950 (main picture) – National Portrait Gallery, London; 27, 36 (top), 38, 41, 52, 53, 94 (Parkinson), 95 (Snowdon),
102 (Parkinson) – Camera Press; 28 top left – Mrs Maureen Yates; 28 top right – Paul Cullen Collection; 28 (centre left &
right), 34 (bottom), 69 (bottom) – *The Illustrated London News* Picture Library; 35 (Bertram Park, 37 (Marcus Adams) –
reproduced by courtesy of Gilbert Adams; 39, 46, 60 (bottom), 61, 64, 65, 70 – BBC Hulton Picture Library; 40 (top), 56 (top
& centre), 58–59 – Copyright reserved, reproduced by Gracious Permission of Her Majesty The Queen; 40 (bottom) – Great
Britain Postcard Club; 42, 72 reproduced by courtesy of the National Postal Museum; 46 (bottom), 47 – Reproduced by
courtesy of Norman Hartnell Ltd and the Trustees of the Victoria and Albert Museum; 48 (top & bottom left) Empress
Elizabeth of Austria and Queen Victoria by Winterhalter – The Bridgeman Art Library; 48 (right) – Norman Hartnell sketch
reproduced by courtesy of Norman Hartnell Ltd; 62 Sketch by Augustus John from *Vogue* 1941; 69 (bottom) – The
Photosource; 71 Queen Elizabeth by Sir James Gunn – Reproduced by courtesy of the Honourable Society of the Middle
Temple; 73 (inset) Sketch for Conversation Piece at the Royal Lodge, Windsor – Mark Fiennes; 83 (right) Queen Elizabeth
the Queen Mother by Cecil Beaton – Private Collection; 84, 85 (top) – Reproduced by courtesy of Central Independent
Television plc; 85 (bottom) – 'Bustino's Special Treat' reproduced by courtesy of Susan Crawford and the Tryon Gallery; 86–
87 – Rex Features; 88, 89 – Elizabeth Johnston; 90–91, 103 – Geoffrey Shakerley; 92–93, 99 – Anwar Hussein; 96, 97, 98 –
Jane Fincher, Photographers International; 100–101 – photographs copyright © Snowdon.

Contents

Queen

isitors to Clarence House present themselves, by appointment, at a small black door just a little to the side.

'Do come in. How very nice to see you. How *very* good of you to come.'

The truth is, of course, that it is very good of Sir Martin Gilliat GCVO, MBE, Private Secretary to Her Majesty Queen Elizabeth the Queen Mother, to let *you* come to Clarence House this rather cold spring morning. It is the Tuesday following the Zeebrugge ferry disaster, and the office has been busy firing off telegrams and letters of condolence to those involved. As Lord Warden of the Cinque Ports, the Queen Mother has a special interest in several of the south coast towns to which the vessel and many of its crew belong.

'One can't help asking oneself what good a telegram can do,' says Sir Martin, 'but people seem to appreciate the gesture.' This remark is left hanging, with no pretence that it solves the problem. Sir Martin clearly wishes he could come up with a better answer.

'Now what will you have to drink? A sherry? A gin and tonic?'

It is only 11.45 a.m., but one visitor's abstemiousness crumbles instantly at the prospect of refreshment in the world headquarters of the gin and tonic. The other visitor is made of sterner stuff, explaining that he does not drink.

'You don't drink at all? Goodness, you'll live for ever!'

For this little joke to strike home, it has to be delivered by the private secretary of a sprightly 87-year-old lady whose evident wellbeing is regularly stimulated, it is no state secret, by the fortifying products of Messrs Gordons and Dubonnet.

Sir Martin picks up a dark crimson cricket ball and twirls it in his fingers. He is a tall, lean man in perpetual motion, chattering and smiling and gesturing. His eyebrows are particularly athletic, doubtless from long years of signalling meaningfully to his employer across rooms and royal enclosures. They vanish heavenwards as he indicates the present location of someone who might otherwise have been a fruitful source of insights into Her Majesty. 'Gathered' is the Clarence House word for old friends who are no more.

The ornaments in Sir Martin's small office include a leather government despatch box, a Rubik cube, a teddy bear and a surprising number of baskets. Clarence House seems to work on these baskets – shallow battered wicker trays in which the correspondence, 140 letters a day on average, gets transferred from office to office.

'It definitely varies with the moon,' says Lady Jean Rankin, who has now been with Her Majesty for forty years. 'Every month, after the full moon, the letters come flooding in.'

Transylvanians may become werewolves, but when the moon is full, British nutcases write to the Queen Mother.

'After you've been reading it all for a little while,' says Lady Jean, 'you begin to wonder whether it is you, perhaps, who is mad, and that they are the sane ones.'

The phone rings. An Irish horsebreeder is going to be at the Gold Cup next week and wonders if there will be any chance of paying his respects to the Queen Mother. He has got some promising three-year-olds he wants to talk about. Sir Martin is very interested.

'Yes,' he says, 'you tell her all about them,' and he makes the arrangements.

'He's already bred Her Majesty one very good horse,' he explains.

Another lady-in-waiting pops her head round the door, just back from a trip to Africa. 'It's terrible,' she says. 'It has completely gone to pot since we left.' Her Majesty will not be surprised at the news. There are modern panic buttons on the walls of Clarence House, intercoms, squawk boxes and electric typewriters in the offices – but this *is* the official residence of the last Empress of India, who retains fond memories of pleasant, leisurely countries with names like Nyasaland, presided over by well-spoken English gentlemen wearing plumed hats.

This does not make her reactionary. Traditional is a better word. During the miners' strike she heard one of her guests refer disparagingly to 'those dreadful miners'.

'I don't know,' said the Queen Mother, 'I've always found them very *loyal*.'

She is the essence of a particular sort of Britishness. If you arrive at Clarence House before the cocktail hour you will be offered tea, coffee or *Bovril*. The day to get the most out of the massed bands and flags of the Royal Tournament is when the Queen Mother has the royal box – and invites Vera Lynn along to sit beside her.

When you meet her – Britain's oldest ever queen, who has to date outlasted Queen Victoria by five years – it is the wide, blue eyes that strike you, like two light blue china saucers. When focused upon a victim, he becomes instantly wobbly at the back of the knees. If you are placed beside her at lunch she will turn her whole body to face you through a full ninety degrees, giving you her attention as if there were no one else at the table, leading the conversation onwards like a good dancer, gently but firmly, and ending her own sentence with little questions – 'Isn't it?', 'Don't you think?' – so that everything moves effortlessly onwards. She seems to be sharing a confidence.

You see it at work as she goes down a reception line. Every so often she throws a fond glance backwards at the man she has just been speaking to – oh, harsh duty, to have torn her away! – and she always does it as she leaves a room, sweeping everyone with a last, warm, regretful farewell. She may well accompany this with her own particular royal gesture, a placing of one open hand on the centre of her bosom, an intimate impulse appropriate only to Queen Mothers and operatic divas of the grandest sort.

She is sensuous – flirtatious even – but in the most decorous way. She understands, leaning over hospital beds, asking questions at a factory bench, or just chit-chatting at a formal reception, that the essential human exchange in all these transactions is not really a question of words and phrases and information, but a matter of *feeling*.

She also understands the importance of style. She *looks* like a Queen. You could never mistake her for anybody else. She is a very familiar face – a very familiar figure, indeed. If one were to draw silhouettes of Britain's queens, there are few that people would recognize instantly – Elizabeth I and Queen Victoria most probably, along with Queen Mary, who might, just possibly, remain familiar to an older generation. The present Queen, Elizabeth II, is still a face, not a statue, and maybe she never will be. But nobody today could fail to recognize the outline of Queen Elizabeth the Queen Mum, and this has been a triumph of style, a style thoughtfully devised and consistently stuck to. She worked out a particular and characteristic look for herself quite soon after she came to the throne in 1936, and she has adhered to that look solidly ever since.

Not that she is solemn or self-important – on the contrary. Everything becomes a party. Is lunch flagging? Let's have a Gray's 'Elegy' competition, see who can remember the most verses – an extra helping of strawberries to the winner. Is it sunny outside? Then let's move the table out under the trees – and then the footmen and pages go into action, and everybody walks out with their glasses across the blue-patched Clarence House lawn, the combined creation of the capital's finest gardeners and her doggy companions.

She lives with rare flourish. Tailors and dressmakers who pin and shape the royal contours in both Clarence House and Buckingham Palace compare the teas. In Clarence House it is tea and cream and scones and jam and cucumber sandwiches with the crusts cut off. In Buckingham Palace it is a pot of tea and a plate of biscuits.

There is nowhere quite like Clarence House, in fact, now left in London – or in Great Britain, for that matter – a grand, elegant, private home, run by the full complement of liveried retainers, a glorious setting for the fine art collected by its owner, and also the heart of a flourishing social life in which judiciously chosen outsiders are brought in to complement a salon of polished and amusing *cavalieri serventi* – Sir Frederick Ashton, Lord Drogheda, Sir Hugh Casson, Sir Alec Guinness, Norman St John-Stevas. There are lunches, dinners, soirées, a tour of the Augustus Johns and the Seago landscapes, a harp recital by Ossian Ellis, some recitation by Dorothy Tutin – or perhaps a tune on the piano from Elton John: 'How *lovely*! It scarcely sounded like a pop song at all.'

The Queen and Prince Philip have never laid claim to a glamorous, extrovert social life. Princess Margaret, since her divorce, had been one of London society's walking wounded. Prince Charles and his wife have proved withdrawn and domestic, disappointing expectations of a sparkling Prince of Wales' set. So it is left to Granny, at the age of eighty-seven, to display the self-confidence and zip, the sheer style, to run a truly royal household – which is why the new recruits, the princesses-to-be out of bedsit land, get popped into Clarence House for a few days at the beginning of their engagement. It is not that she runs a royal charm school: the Queen Mother does not, sadly, give courses in waving, or prescribe the correct number of inches for a decolletage – as has, on occasions, been glaringly apparent. The new girls are sent to stay with her because she is the head of the family, and because she has become with the years the very essence of royalness. Queen Elizabeth the Queen Mother is the supreme exponent of a particular sort of magic on which the whole institution of monarchy depends, a summation of history and charm and patriotism and sentimentality which has made her over the years into a unique national treasure. It is instructive for young princesses to study this – and it is instructive for the rest of us as well.

here's not a man in England today who doesn't envy him,' recorded Chips Channon in his diary for 16 January 1923, the day it was announced that Prince Albert, Duke of York, second son of King George V and Queen Mary, had won the hand of the Lady Elizabeth Bowes Lyon, youngest daughter of the Earl and Countess of Strathmore. 'The clubs are in gloom.'

Channon, a young American who was working very hard in the early 1920s at becoming a member of British society, always reckoned himself a little bit in love with the Lady Elizabeth Bowes Lyon. So did a lot of other men. There was something so vulnerable and old-fashioned about her. Her voice had a peculiar, emotional quality – musical, with an appealing catch in it. She was pretty, sensual almost, in a wistful way, with big round eyes and her dark hair pulled back into the bun that she still wears today. She was not stuffy. The Lady Elizabeth was rather good fun, in fact – flirtatious even. But you would not dream of presuming on the invitation.

'Holding hands in a boat, that was her idea of courting,' were the famous words of her friend in those days, Helen Cecil. Lord Strathmore's gentle daughter was different, somehow, from other young ladies of her generation – close-bobbed and brittle as a breed, rather fiercely made up. You could imagine having quite a fling with one of them.

But Elizabeth Bowes Lyon was the object of more tender, settling down-style fantasies, the sort of partner you could visualize as a soothing companion, a home-maker, a marvellous mother. And so, indeed, she was to prove as wife to Prince Albert, 'Bertie', Duke of York.

The House of Windsor loved her. She had such a capacity for smiling. She brought laughter and good humour to a family not noted, hitherto, for either – a certain softness, a definite grace. She knew how to bring out the sprightly side of the formidable Queen Mary, and she swept the gruff King George V right off his feet. 'The better I know and the more I see of your dear little wife,' he wrote to Bertie shortly after the marriage, 'the more charming I think she is.'

Her children, born in 1926 and 1930, made her even more beloved. Motherliness became a component of her appeal from quite an early date. Until the arrival of the Princesses Elizabeth and Margaret Rose the royal family had been comparatively childless – a gap in their own lives and also in their public persona, since the patter of tiny feet in Palace corridors not only brings pleasure to the Palace inhabitants, but can provide a potent element in the appeal of a bourgeois monarchy. So it proved with the little princesses, who were welcomed with joy by King George V and Queen Mary, and by the country as a whole. In fact, the two little girls became the object of something of a cult.

Their mother was both the inspiration and, in some senses, the impresario of this. She loved being a mother – with the help of the odd maid and nanny. She was not permissive. The little princesses were invariably well-behaved. But she had ideas about childrearing that were considered 'modern' in their day. She believed that education should be fun – lots of romps and games and fresh air and dogs. Every new day should bring something new, a visit here, a picnic there. She was, actually, not that much concerned with conventional examination subjects. Her elder daughter's syllabus had to be stiffened up after 1936, when it became clear that the little girl really was in line for the throne. But Elizabeth, Duchess of York, brought freshness, humanity and warmth to the hitherto sterile process of raising royal children.

She was understandably proud of this, and allowed the world a glimpse of life inside 145 Piccadilly, the Yorks' London home, in two books published in the early 1930s – *The Story of Princess Elizabeth*, by Anne Ring, a former secretary to the Duchess, and *The Married Life of Her Royal Highness the Duchess of York*, by Lady Cynthia Asquith, 'Written and Published with the PERSONAL APPROVAL of Her Royal Highness'. Readers were taken up to the nursery floor, saw the rocking-horse on the landing, could almost touch the little scarlet brushes and dustpans 'with which every morning the little princesses sweep the thick pile carpet', and heard the screams and splashes through the bathroom door where the Duke, a man, was actually bathing his daughters.

These books, both bestsellers which went through numerous editions and regular updating over the years, were the 1930s' equivalent of the 'intimate' television films which have proved such bolsters of monarchical sentiment since the first screening of 'The Royal Family' in 1969, and they revealed another side to the smiling Duchess of York – her shrewd grasp of public relations. Nothing quite so graphic and intimate had ever been published about living members of the royal family with royal approval – and it was very royal approval, since the books could not possibly have appeared without the sanction and encouragement of King George V and Queen Mary. Elizabeth Bowes Lyon had been rash enough on the first, joyous flush of her engagement day in January 1923 to grant an interview to an enterprising representative of the *Star* who presented himself at her parents' front door, and she had been royally rapped over the knuckles for it by her father-in-law. She has not given an interview about herself from that day to this.

The King and Queen, however, thoroughly approved of the cosy, domestic existence that the Duke and Duchess of York had created with their little daughters, and they evidently felt that its example should be propagated. Since the reign of Queen Victoria, British royal life had been taking on more and more everyday, bourgeois characteristics, both in reality and, even more, in the image presented to the general public. The small York family unit took this a stage further. King George V and Queen Mary prided themselves on their own domesticity, but their family had been large and extended. Here at 145 Piccadilly, just a few yards away from a bus stop, was the first small, royal, nuclear family unit – a neat, hardworking, quiet husband, an adoring mother with a lovely smile, and the well-behaved little girls, just two of them, in ankle socks – a model of dreamlike domesticity, for all the world, as John Pearson has remarked, like the characters in an Ovaltine advertisement.

Such a picture could not help but reinforce the identity between the royal family and the increasingly middle-class, suburban character of Britain in the 1930s – and as the decade progressed, there was some need of reinforcement, for even as the Duchess of York's modern ideas moved in one direction, so those of her brother-in-law, the Prince of Wales – Edward to the world and David to his family – were moving in another. He was greatly concerned with being modern was Edward, Prince of Wales: smoking in public, wearing loud sweaters, frequenting night clubs – and he made much of his wish to do away with the mumbo jumbo of monarchy and to drag it into the twentieth century. But King George V felt that David was heading down the wrong track. A sounder, more rooted royal style was being evolved by his second son, Bertie, with the help of his wife Elizabeth, Duchess of York.

ld Queen Mary took great pride in her photograph albums – large, red, leather-bound volumes, each of them bearing her private childhood signature, May, embossed in gold in the top right-hand corner, with a delicate gilt coronet set above. They live today in the Round Tower at Windsor Castle, twenty-nine volumes, each of them packed, page after page, with postcard-sized photographs which the Queen captioned herself and laid out chronologically, side by side, to form a graphic narrative. The design of the pages would seem to owe not a little to that of the *Illustrated London News* – and sprinkled amid the family snaps there are, indeed, a number of photographs which come from that very publication, since Her Majesty was in the habit of scanning the press and then ordering up copies of the pictures she needed to create her own peculiarly symbolic version of her family history.

It is volume 27 which contains the moment of truth – the years 1935, 1936 and 1937. The Queen has written these dates on the inside of the front cover in her thin, spidery hand, and through the mixture of public and private images which follow, she recounts the story of the British monarchy's crisis years.

On the first page is the reassuring presence of the old King, Queen Mary's husband, George V, trimly bearded and moustached in white spats and shooting suit. May 6th, 1935, was the date of his Silver Jubilee, but he is looking rather frail. He is puffy around the eyes, and by the autumn he is looking still worse. 'G. leaving Ballater after his last visit to Balmoral 27th Sept'. The old King is muffled up in a bowler hat and overcoat, leaning on a walking stick as he inspects a squad of kilted soldiers in the thin September sunlight. He says farewell to the album in a couple of re-runs of his Silver Jubilee, photographs which the Queen had had printed up especially large, and then inserted, out of chronological sequence, to provide a meaningful end to a chapter. The King is stretching out of a carriage, symbolically yielding up a jewelled sword – to the Lord Mayor of London, as it happens, not to his son.

There are no photographs at all of George V's great state funeral – no pictures of anything, in fact, for the opening months of January, February and March 1936. The story resumes with a photograph of the dead monarch's pet parrot, Charlotte, making the best of life, apparently, without her master. Then, as the spring gains momentum, Queen Mary makes an effort to record some of the details of the new reign of her eldest son David, King Edward VIII.

Things are not the same. For the previous twenty-five years the Queen's albums have shown her at Balmoral every August and September, walking the moors, entertaining guests, picnicking. But in 1936 her September pages are filled with sepia postcards of interesting country houses – Harewood, Hovingham, Wortley Hall, visits which she made in the course of a tour of Yorkshire – for the new King is in residence at Balmoral this autumn, and the hostess of the royal house party is an American lady, Mrs Wallis Simpson.

The Armistice ceremony at the Cenotaph on 11 November 1936 fills a page or two, for here is David doing something kingly for a change, dressed in uniform and laying wreaths in company with his younger brothers, led by Bertie, Duke of York. But just one month later, to the day, it is all over. At the bottom of a right-hand page, side by side, are stuck two press photographs of speeding cars. Flashlights catch the wheel hubs. The cars move too quickly for the blurred, behatted figures in the back seats to be easily recognized. But Queen Mary can pick out the features of her two eldest sons, so similar in some ways and yet so different. 'Bertie Dec 11th after David's abdication' reads one caption. The other reads 'David leaving England!' And then the page turns on to yet another new reign.

It was a bad time. 'The thin-faced 30s', Compton MacKenzie called them. The depression was far from over in December 1936, and war was already on the way: gas-proof prams were unveiled by the Air Raids Precautions Department on 20 December. Small wonder that people were taking refuge in fantasy – cinemas were opening at the rate of two a week. But the greatest fantasy of all had let people down.

Britain went into mourning twice in 1936, the first time for the death of King George V, and a second time, more painfully, for the abdication of his eldest son, since the departure of Edward VIII was rather like a funeral – and, in its emptiness, it was in some ways harder to bear, since what had passed away was nothing physical. It was, more achingly, an idea that had died – the enchantment generated by the glittering young Prince of Wales, the dream of Edward VIII as a bright, handsome, generous king. It now turned out that he was a smaller man. He had shown a certain nobility in consenting to his own legal death, in going quietly. But with that act he had also confessed to a selfishness and imperfection which people expect royal persons to rise above. Britons were shocked to discover in 1936 that Edward VIII could love anything more than being their king.

They could not say the same of the new King and Queen. Duty was their watchword, and always had been. There was no doubt about that. But they were still, in people's minds, the Yorks, the reserve team. Had they the glamour, the dash to provide the substance of a dream?

The new Queen Elizabeth accomplished the task more easily. During the abdication crisis itself she succumbed to illness – a not uncommon reaction, throughout her life, to moments of great stress. But by the middle of December 1936, she was up again and fulfilling her new responsibilities with authentic queenliness. Her mother-in-law's photograph album shows her coming down the steps of 145 Piccadilly early in 1937, light and elegant in shades of pastel, waving and smiling, a very picture of regality. She is often described as a reluctant queen, and the evidence suggests that, in anticipation, she had been. In the weeks leading up to the abdication she and Bertie truly shrank from the throne. There was nothing predatory about them, no sensing of their own advantage in the catastrophe. But here she is, within weeks of her accession, and before the holy oil has struck, positively swelling and blossoming with sovereignty. It is, suddenly, clear that this lady is Queen Elizabeth, as if she were born, raised and destined to be nothing else.

The Duke of York found it rather more difficult to become King George VI. It had been a happy thought to take his father's name as king, a reassuring touch of continuity. But his need was also to break away, to create some sort of identity for himself, and this was not so easy, for the influence of his mother and father had been to smother, not bring out, the sensitive, rather wise and caring spirit that lay within. 'The House of Hanover,' said Owen Morshead, the royal librarian, 'like ducks, produce bad parents. They trample on their young.'

The most obvious sign of this in the new King George VI was his stammer, and the mixture of shyness and frustrated temper that accompanied it. His official biographer says that the stammering only started when Prince Albert was six or seven, and suggests that it may have been connected with the boy being naturally left-handed and being compelled by his tutors to write with his right. The Prince spent long painful hours of his childhood wearing splints designed to correct a tendency to knock-knees. He had to do his reading and writing at a special invalid table, and these physical constraints were combined with the psychological burden of his father's frequent criticism and reproof. 'Now that you are five years old,' George V had written to him on his birthday in December 1900, 'I hope you will always try & be obedient & do at once what you are told, as you will find it will come much easier to you the sooner you begin.'

Prince Albert, Duke of York was not, in the eyes of many, a very impressive young man. His public utterances were paralysed by long, embarrassing pauses – 'God's curse on me,' was how he morosely described his stammer – and he vented his depression on those close to him in fierce fits of temper, which courtiers in later years came to refer to as his 'gnashes'.

'Behave yourself, Sir,' would snap Louis Greig, the young military surgeon who was given the often difficult job of being minder to the prince in his bachelor days.

This graceless, prickly Bertie was, we may presume, the character that the Lady Elizabeth Bowes Lyon turned down when he first proposed to her in the early 1920s. She had other suitors, some very eligible young men. One of them, James Stuart, son of the 17th Earl of Moray, was the epitome of everything Bertie was not – self-assured, debonair, forceful. But James Stuart lacked constancy. He played the field. While Bertie, by contrast, in his continuing suit, demonstrated staunchness, fidelity and pluck.

'I have always found him a very straight and honourable boy,' the Prince's tutor had written as he sent him off to naval school at the age of thirteen, 'very kind-hearted and generous.'

This, as she grew to know him, was the side of Prince Bertie which Elizabeth Bowes Lyon came to appreciate, and in due course, to love. She saw something in him that so many other people did not, and in seeing it, she helped make it come true. Elizabeth Bowes Lyon, wooed three times and finally won, was Prince Bertie's first great triumph in a life not noted hitherto for its successes. She believed in him, and under the warming influence of her faith, a delicate and rather fine persona found better ways than temper to assert itself. In their marriage she gave him her strength in quite an old-fashioned, sacrificial sort of way, and he repaid her with softness and devotion – a total, almost slavish adoration such as few ordinary men, let alone kings, are willing to yield up.

They operated as a team. When, in 1926, the Duke of York finally found the speech specialist, Lionel Logue, who promised a real answer for his stammering, he went through the therapy with the Duchess at his side, the two of them practising together the breathing techniques by which Logue helped achieve relaxation. Peter Townsend was a boy at Haileybury when the Duke of York, speaking at the opening of the school's new dining hall, faltered and stopped as he started. The boys tensed with embarrassment. But the Duchess kept smiling. She seemed to whisper to her husband, 'willing him over the wall of silence and into the next sentence. Her sense of partnership was sublime.'

When Townsend entered the royal service a dozen years later as equerry to King George VI he became privy to the more intimate side of the partnership, the skill with which the Queen knew how to defuse her husband's sudden bursts of ill temper. She could exert such a tranquillizing effect. She knew how to divert him, heading him off from confrontation, and when he did explode, she was quite unflustered.

'Oh Bertie,' she would say, then feel for his pulse and pretend to count like a clock – tick, tick, tick. The anger would just drain away.

Today Her Majesty Queen Elizabeth refutes the suggestion that her late husband – 'the King' as she still refers to him, almost in the present tense – was an incomplete personality. To her he was wise and loving and understanding and strong. He was everything that a husband and father and king should be. She loved him and depended on him, and there is no need to dispute her memory, since its deep reality came to be shared by millions of his subjects. As people heard the voice of the quiet and diffident George VI wrestling so tangibly with his speech affliction, they came to see in him the qualities of perseverance that Elizabeth Bowes Lyon had sensed – the hard, dutiful, honest core to the man, which she loved and which they came to love as well.

The history of the British royal family since the reign of Queen Victoria has, in many ways, been a story of strong-willed, powerful women, and the events which unexpectedly brought King George VI to the throne can very much be seen in that light. Both Bertie and his elder brother, David, were dependent on their women, looking to them in adult life for the mothering they had never had. But whereas Mrs Simpson un-kinged her man, the new Queen Elizabeth, working in a softer, more subtle fashion, proved to be the making of hers. She was to contribute much in her own right to the lustre of the British monarchy, but her greatest achievement was to help make her husband into a great King.

hen the Duke and Duchess of York had first realized how serious the abdication crisis was getting, and that it really might lead to them having to take over the throne, they went down on their knees, it was reported, to pray together that the cup might pass from them. Then, when their prayer was not granted, they knelt again, to acknowledge their acceptance of God's will.

Religion. Religion. It was tied up into the magic of monarchy. It seemed to matter more than ever, in an increasingly godless age, that national figureheads should partake of the divine. It was one reason, thought Stanley Baldwin – perhaps the basic reason – why Edward VIII just would not do.

'He lacks religion,' the Prime Minister confided in Harold Nicolson. 'I told his mother so. I said to her "Ma'am, the King has no religious sense."'

The coronation of King George VI and Queen Elizabeth in May 1937 was to confirm how powerfully an avowedly rational society could be moved by intangible things. In one sense it was a colossal sham. The new king was not being crowned by the Grace of God and hundreds of years of national tradition, but by the grace of Stanley Baldwin and the House of Commons who had not liked his predecessor's taste in women. But few people chose to see it that way. If the abdication had been a wound, a rending of the national fabric, the ancient, half-pagan mysteries of the coronation which followed less than six months later were to prove a salve, a national healing in which ritual, ceremony, sentiment, a day off work, and – for the first time – live radio, all helped work their varied magic. In 1953 the coronation of Queen Elizabeth II was to stand for regeneration, a new age. In May 1937 the theme was reassurance, continuity, a return to old, safe ways.

As May 1937 approached, the demands of the ritual brought home to the new Queen Elizabeth how the sacredness of her new position was no abstraction. It affected her very person. She had to have her ears pierced to do full justice to the jewels that were now tokens of her majesty. She changed her hairstyle at this time, pulling it back off her forehead – no more fringe, or wisps. She had always had an instinct for tradition. Now she partnered this with the regal frame of thinking in which the smallest gestures take on meaning. Her husband bestowed the Order of the Garter upon her, and she chose to pin its broad blue band upon her shoulder with the pearl and diamond Jubilee brooch which Queen Victoria was given by her household.

She was very conscious that hers was only a supporting role. Well aware of her potency in public – the magical, rather exciting power that she could exert to stir a crowd – she made a deliberate decision, according to Dermot Morrah, the writer and constitutional expert who was in the royal couple's confidence in these years, not to upstage the King. As she had worked with Bertie through the breathing therapies of Lionel Logue, so she now rehearsed every step of the coronation ceremonial with him, side by side. On the night of Sunday 9 May 1937, the couple concluded their long weeks of preparation in a private meeting with the Archbishop of Canterbury in Buckingham Palace.

'They knelt with me,' recalled the Archbishop later. 'I prayed for them and for their realm and Empire, and I gave them my personal blessing. I was much moved, and so were they. Indeed there were tears in their eyes when we rose from our knees.'

Several witnesses of the ceremony in Westminster Abbey three days later have recorded how the sacramental aura emanating from the King and Queen was almost tangible. Watching them ride out on their great day from a window in Buckingham Palace, Dorothy Wilding, whose photographs of the robed and crowned couple were to play their own role in the propagation of the pageant, found herself overcome with unexpected emotion. 'My arms went all gooseflesh,' she remembered, 'thrilled to the marrow with singing pride in the old British Empire.'

There were long periods during the coronation ceremony, George VI confided afterwards to Ramsay MacDonald, when he was unaware of what was happening around him. Both the King and Queen were so moved by the ritual purification and transformation through which they passed that they fell for a period into a trance.

Talking later with Queen Elizabeth, Ramsay MacDonald remarked upon the transformation. The King, he told her, had 'come on magnificently since his accession'.

Her Majesty was delighted.

'And am I doing all right?' she asked.

'Oh you . . .' the old politician replied, and he gave a broad sweep with his arm to show that, in her, he took all that for granted.

n 28 May 1937, two weeks and two days after the coronation of King George VI and Queen Elizabeth, the *London Gazette* announced that, by Letters Patent issued under the Great Seal of the Realm, the Duke of Windsor would henceforward be entitled to 'the title, style or attribute of Royal Highness' – but that his wife, the Duchess, did not qualify for the same dignity. What this meant in practical terms was that people who came in contact with the new Duchess of Windsor were not supposed to address her as 'Your Royal Highness', but as 'Your Grace'. Neither were they supposed to bow or bob to her.

From such deprivation developed schism and bitterness to rival that between Montague and Capulet, for the Duchess of Windsor correctly interpreted this act of apartheid, Debrett-style, as a slur on her character – and the person whom she came to blame most vehemently, over the years, for this and for a number of other slights, real and imagined, was her sister-in-law, Queen Elizabeth. When James Pope-Hennessy met the Duchess of Windsor in 1958 he noticed how she had a special facial expression 'reserved for speaking of the Queen Mother', and that this expression – a 'contortion' he called it – was 'very unpleasant to behold.'

The popular folk memory has tended to take its cue from this and from various other signs of the bitterness that the Duchess of Windsor took no pains to conceal, to cultivate the notion of a 'Royal Feud' between the Duchess and Queen Elizabeth, thus proposing the intriguing possibility of a dark and angry side to the ever-smiling Queen Mum. This would, of course, also prove that she is human.

Mrs Simpson first met her future sister-in-law one weekend in 1936 when the Prince of Wales took her over to Royal Lodge, the Windsor weekend home of the Duke and Duchess of York. In later years she was to recall her welcome that spring afternoon as displaying a noticeable absence of the overbrimming love and kindliness for which the Duchess of York was so celebrated – and Mrs Simpson was probably quite correct. As a communicant member of the Church of Scotland, Elizabeth Bowes Lyon had been brought up with backbone, to tell the difference between right and wrong. As a great aristocrat's daughter, she also knew what would do and what would not.

The abdication itself intensified her feelings, but her own emotions were in no way stronger than those of her husband, George VI, or of her mother-in-law, Queen Mary. In May 1937 the entire royal family was still absolutely furious with Mrs Simpson, not just because of the recent past, but because she also promised to be a source of scandal and embarrassment, so far as they could see, for the continuing future. Queen Elizabeth the Queen Mother does not like unpleasantness. In the late 1960s Ludovic Kennedy was sitting with her in Clarence House, discussing a possible television programme on the subject of her life, when the question of the abdication came up.

'I am afraid I just can't talk about it,' she said.

'But Ma'am,' argued Kennedy, 'your whole life hinged on it.'

'Yes, I know,' she replied, 'but I just can't.'

The programme was never made. 1936, the abdication, Mrs Simpson, the HRH business, it is all wrapped up for her in distress, tension and worry that she would rather just forget. She lived through it, she did her best for Bertie, for the throne and for the country, and she does not see the point of digging up old pain. You do not waste your time brooding if you are in the business of sunshine and light – though Her Majesty has on occasions in recent years been overheard to muse, almost to herself, in mild complaint at the popular notion that she waged a personal vendetta against Wallis.

'I didn't hate her. I just felt sorry for her.'

Only a lady of a certain seniority, surrounded by adoring courtiers, friends and relatives, could pass a comment like this and hope to get away with it, for while it may well reflect her fellow feeling in later years for the lonely, widowed Duchess, it bears no possible relationship to what she must have thought in 1936 in the dark days of abdication, or in 1952 when her own husband died, his fragile health additionally strained by the worries and responsibilities of a job he had not asked for. When someone commented to her some time before the war on the excellent job that the Duchess of Windsor had done for the Duke – no more drinking, no more pouches under his eyes – the Queen was distinctly unimpressed.

'Yes,' she remarked, 'who has the lines under his eyes now?'

The fateful decision over the Duchess of Windsor's non-royal status was made in the weeks surrounding the coronation, and the sacramental fervour of that ceremony must have played its part – for how could one swear solemn oaths, kneel in homage to age-old verities, and pledge allegiance to sacred trusts, then casually bestow this same sacerdotal dignity upon a person who had threatened it so direly? Dignity was dignity. If you care about something deeply, forgiveness, sometimes, can be just another compromise.

This is why, ultimately, Queen Elizabeth the Queen Mother may be right when she implies that her animus against the Duchess of Windsor was not fundamentally personal. As Queen Consort of King George VI, she believed in and cared deeply for the purity and value of her husband's sacred trust – the reflection of which the Duchess of Windsor so desperately wished to enjoy. As wife of Bertie, the shy, stammering Duke of York, so long in the shadow of his talented elder brother, she was entitled to be happy when the row over the Duchess's status inhibited the Duke from coming back to England to rekindle his public magic.

People who are close to Queen Elizabeth the Queen Mother all talk about the same thing. Beneath her charm and softness, they say, there lies a very solid, basic steeliness, a quite unequivocal refusal to compromise on the things that really matter, and as they try to describe it, they all tend to put it in the same way, with a reliance on cliché which suggests they are more comfortable with the softness than with what lies underneath: 'There's an iron fist in the velvet glove,' they say.

oyal fashion is not the height of fashion. It is a game played by rules that are all its own – signs and tokens which appear to bear a resemblance to the clothes that the rest of the world is wearing, but which actually indicate the otherness of the royal person who is wearing them: the hat, the gloves, the colours that are only worn by ordinary ladies when dressed up for a wedding – plus the overlarge handbag resolutely carried everywhere, despite the spare hands of a lady-in-waiting.

Elizabeth, Duchess of York, was never noted as a fashion plate. Her hems floated up and down through the 1920s and '30s, trailing in pursuit of Paris and Mayfair at a decorous distance. She liked things trimmed with fur – some osprey fronds, perhaps, a little netting. Her clothes were pretty and charming and rather on the wispy side. They did not compare with the pared-down elegance of Princess Marina, Duchess of Kent, or the metallic chic of Mrs Simpson, and they did not pretend to. The Duchess of York sought her identity in other directions. She was content to surrender the drift of her wardrobe to the woman who had made her wedding dress in 1923, Madame Handley Seymour, a court dressmaker of the old school who had Frenchified her name – Madame was, in reality, a plain English Mrs – and whose most important customer was Queen Mary.

It was Madame Handley Seymour who got the commission for the new Queen Elizabeth's coronation dress in May 1937. She was tried and trusted. No one was in the mood to take risks in the early months of 1937. But the new Queen had quite recently been attracted by the work of an ambitious young English designer, Norman Hartnell, who had made a name providing clothes for West End shows and for theatrical folk – Gertrude Lawrence and Evelyn Laye were among his clients. So early in January 1937 Hartnell was summoned to Buckingham Palace to discuss the dresses of the six maids of honour who would carry the train of the Queen's heavy coronation robes, and he was told that he should also start thinking about some formal outfits that Her Majesty would need for other occasions. Afterwards the King took the young designer for a stroll through the State Apartments.

George VI had been thinking quite seriously about the style of his coronation. To illustrate the look he wanted for his wife's maids of honour, he had invited Hartnell to study a painting of the coronation of his great-grandmother, Queen Victoria. The train-bearers were shown wearing head-wreaths of gilded wheat, and the King and Queen were both agreed that this was a feature they would like to imitate. But what followed now, as George VI led Hartnell through the Palace corridors, cigarette in hand, was a notion that appears to have sprung unaided from the new king's own head.

George VI stopped in front of some paintings by Franz Xaver Winterhalter, the German artist whose flowing, dreamlike representations of beautiful women had made him the rage at courts all over Europe in the middle of the nineteenth century, and he told Hartnell that that was how he would like his wife, Queen Elizabeth, to look. 'His Majesty made it clear in his quiet way,' recorded Hartnell later, 'that I should attempt to capture this picturesque grace in the dresses I was to design for the Queen.'

Winterhalter's rhapsodic and sometimes quite erotic imagery must have been part of Prince Bertie's mental wallpaper from an early age. Queen Victoria had had a passion for the artist, who also gave her painting lessons. Victoria commissioned over a hundred Winterhalters in the 1840s and '50s, plus numerous copies of his portraits, and, hanging all over Buckingham Palace and Windsor, they provided the context of royalty in which Bertie grew up. The future George VI never saw himself as an artistic fellow – if anything he was rather the reverse. But Winterhalter's vision of royal womanhood evidently stirred something in his spirit, for when prompted to fantasize about the woman he loved, it was in Winterhalter's ethereal terms that he saw her.

Hartnell went back to his workroom thinking crinoline – the name comes from the stiff horsehair, *crin* in French, used with whalebone or metal hoops to puff out a Victorian petticoat. It was not Hartnell's intention simply to copy a mid-Victorian costume. An 1860s' waistline was sharp and high by 1930s' tastes. But by smoothing the dress down over the hips, and making much use of light, floating gauze and embroidery, Hartnell achieved an effect that was both contemporary and also redolent of the romantic nineteenth-century empresses whom George VI admired so much. (The 'Winterhalters' that the King had particularly pointed out to Hartnell in January 1937, portraits of the Empress Eugénie of France and the Empress Elizabeth of Austria, were both, in fact, copies of originals that hung elsewhere.)

It was nearly a year before the results of Hartnell's work were first seen. The Queen stayed true to Madame Handley Seymour for the receptions and banquets of the coronation season. But in November 1937, the vision of a modern Winterhalter finally bore fruit in the dress which the Queen wore to the State banquet in honour of the visiting King Leopold III of the Belgians – a stunning confection of gleaming silver tissue, running in and out at the waist and then blossoming out over over a hooped crinoline of stiffened silver gauze. Hartnell had given his theatricality full rein. Slashed across with the blue Garter riband and diamond star, the Winterhalter Queen could have stepped up into one of the paintings on the walls of the State Apartments and vanished. Queen Elizabeth had a look of her own at last – not like her mother-in-law, not like Princess Marina, and especially not like Wallis Simpson. She was floating, feminine, soft and even sensual – but she was every inch a Queen. The echoes of Victoria were most reassuring. When the time came to choose the outfits for the State visit to Paris the following year, it was Hartnell whom Queen Elizabeth commissioned to execute her entire wardrobe, some thirty grand dresses, plus coats, wraps, stoles and parasols – and Madame Handley Seymour had to make do with the patronage of Queen Mary.

If Queen Elizabeth, in a supportive and inspirational sense, helped to 'make' King George, it can also be said that he, in his fruitful and somewhat surprising walk through the State Apartments with Norman Hartnell, helped to define and make his wife the Queen who was to become fixed so vividly in her subjects' imagination in 1937 – and has remained there ever since.

It is a potent thing, the royal 'image', far more than a matter of mere surface appeal. Holbein's four square portraits of Henry VIII, or Van Dyck's eerie, wasted vision of the martyr Charles, have come to 'be' those kings because, in each case, the look says something accurate and characteristic about the man, capturing an essence that has made the image a reality – *the* reality, in fact. So King George VI's loving fantasy of his wife, inspired by the *légerdemain* of a Victorian court painter, then turned into white tulle and sequins by a Bruton Street fashion designer, has come to be Queen Elizabeth not so much because it is singular – which it is – but because it conjures in the mind's eye a vision of warmth, femininity, fantasy and reassurance which we feel to be the truth.

The Winterhalter Queen got her first public outing in Paris in the summer of 1938, in a visit that is still recalled by the French with some awe. When Diana, the Princess of Wales, visited France soon after her marriage in the early 1980s, local comment was quite kind. But more than one observer remarked that the young princess's dresses could hardly be compared with those sported so stunningly by her grandmother-in-law nearly half a century before.

Queen Elizabeth's mother, Lady Strathmore, had died in June 1938, even as the State visit was due to begin, and this seemed, for a moment, to threaten a sombre wardrobe of purple or black. But it was happily remembered that white could also be a colour of royal mourning. In a final flourish of her prerogative, Queen Victoria had insisted on a white funeral, having spent most of her existence in black. So the trip was set back a week or so, Hartnell got to work, and within a fortnight every single one of Queen Elizabeth's outfits – silks, satins, velvet, cloth, taffeta, tulle, chiffon and lace – everything was white.

The effect was dazzling. 'We saw the King and Queen from a window,' wrote Lady Diana Cooper, 'coming down the Champs Elysées, with roofs, windows and pavements roaring exultantly.'

This was more than an ordinary courtesy visit. There was panic in the air. War was little more than a year away in the summer of 1938, and at times it seemed even closer. Hitler was on the verge of invading Czechoslovakia, provoking the Munich crisis. So quite a high proportion of the ceremonial in Paris that summer had a military character: wreath-layings, parades, flypasts – ripostes, all of them, to the grim pageantry of Nuremberg. A shimmer of poise and serenity did not go amiss.

The visit was a personal triumph for Norman Hartnell, who had tried once before to launch himself in Paris, and had failed dismally. Now the plaudits were unanimous and quite sincere. Hartnell was made an *Officier d'Académie*. Taking fashion to France was a daring gesture. Who would have dreamt that the modest couple whom the smart set were describing, only a year or so earlier, as the 'dreary Yorks', could have pulled off such a dashing *succès d'estime* – actually setting the trends? When Queen Elizabeth attended a garden party at the Bagatelle, trailing her white, cobweb dress across the green lawn, she happened to open up her parasol of transparent lace. At a stroke, noted Hartnell, the fortunes of the parasol makers of London and Paris were transformed.

he new-look Queen Elizabeth was guaranteed approval when she arrived in North America in the spring of 1939. *Gone with the Wind* was the film of the year, and both the United States and Canada were awash with nostalgia for the 1860s.

The tour started in Quebec in May, the first time that a reigning sovereign had visited one of the dominions, and the first example of the sort of royal tour that has since become routine. King George V and Queen Mary did not travel any more than they had to. Nor did they loosen their regal remoteness when they did. But in Ottawa in 1939, having just laid the foundation stone of the new Supreme Court Building, Queen Elizabeth heard that some of the stone masons came from Scotland, and she took the King away from the official party to talk to them, spending an unscheduled ten minutes in Scottish reminiscence. Later, at the unveiling of the War Memorial, she again struck off into the crowd, wandering and chatting with some of the thousands of veterans who were there.

'Walkabout' is an Australian word applied to royal progresses in the reign of Queen Elizabeth II, but it was in Ottawa in May 1939 that this informal chatting and wandering was first practised by a reigning British king or queen. 'She has a perfect genius for the right kind of publicity,' enthused the Canadian Governor-General, Lord Tweedsmuir, and King George VI thoroughly approved. 'There must be no more high-hat business,' he remarked to one of his advisers during the tour, 'the sort of thing that my father and those of his day regarded as essential.' There should be more of this coming into contact with ordinary people, much more of 'the common touch'. This, thought the King, represented 'a new idea of kingship'.

Informality went a stage further when the royal couple reached the United States, where they had been invited by President Roosevelt to spend a quiet weekend at his Hyde Park home. The President offered his guests a repast of cold beer and hot dogs, then everyone changed their clothes and dived into the pool. It all proved rather confusing to Americans' ideas of how a King and Queen should be. Eleanor Roosevelt, who had evidently been studying photographs of the Paris tour, carefully dusted off a long dress for the royal arrival – only to see Queen Elizabeth turn up in an outfit that descended no lower than the knee.

Roosevelt's anglophobe, isolationist critics saw politics at work. They rightly suspected the visit as part of a British attempt to secure US support in their coming conflict with the dictators. For that reason, FDR had advised against the British Foreign Secretary, Lord Halifax, accompanying the tour. But the simplicity and sincerity of the apparently apolitical king and queen tied the critics' hands most effectively. It was difficult to read anything very sinister into hot-dog eating. The royal couple disarmed suspicion. Vast crowds turned out to welcome them, press comment was adulatory, and although in a poll after the tour, 24 per cent of those who were questioned retained fears of being enticed into a warlike alliance, 58 per cent agreed that the visit had been 'no more than a token of friendship among English-speaking peoples'.

George VI and his Queen arrived back in Southampton to a hero's welcome. Delirious crowds packed the quay. People had been following the royal progress through the illustrated magazines and newspapers, and they were as entranced by the hot dogs as the Americans had been. The tour had been a triumph, achieving all and more than had been hoped for, and giving George VI and Queen Elizabeth the international stature that only American exposure can. People felt proud of what their shy King and his little wife had achieved, and the doubts that had hung over the abilities of the reserve team in 1936 now contributed to the respect accorded their achievement. The stuttering, diffident Bertie had become a poised, impressive monarch. The motherly Duchess had become a glamorous Queen. Those close to the court particularly appreciated the way that Queen Elizabeth had done it – calming, relaxing, encouraging – working to build up a partnership with her loved one, not diminishing, which is what Svengalis do.

Their reception in London, incredibly, rivalled the euphoria of Coronation Day, huge crowds lining the streets from Waterloo where the boat train came in. With war now only weeks away, emotions were running very high. The House of Commons broke off from its debates, and the MPs came out on to the pavement to join in the cheers.

'They went very slowly,' wrote Harold Nicolson in his diary for 23 June 1939, 'and there were the King and Queen and the two princesses. We lost all our dignity and yelled and yelled. The King wore a happy schoolboy grin. The Queen was superb. She really does manage to convey to each individual in the crowd that he or she has had a personal greeting. It is due, I think, to the brilliance of her eyes... She is in truth one of the most amazing Queens since Cleopatra.'

The politicians filed back into the chamber, and as they went, wrote Nicolson, there were lumps in their throats.

Elizabeth
Bowes Lyon

*E*lizabeth Bowes Lyon, aged 4, at her mother's knee, with her father, Lord Strathmore (wearing cap), her elder sisters and her six brothers (the youngest, David, sitting on his mother's lap). The photograph was taken in 1904. Below, aged 9, with her pony, Bobs, in the garden of St Paul's Walden Bury – her family's Hertfordshire home, where Prince Bertie, Duke of York, later proposed to her and was accepted. Right, aged 8, painted by Mabel Hankey.

*F*irst pose. Elizabeth Bowes Lyon,
aged 4, and (right) aged 7.

'The clubs are in gloom'

THE ROYAL WEDDING

ALL HAPPINESS ATTEND THEM.

PHOTO.
CENTRAL NEWS.   H. M. QUEEN MARY,   116.C.
BEAGLES POSTCARDS.
T.R.H. THE DUKE & DUCHESS OF YORK.

*W*edding day. Elizabeth Bowes Lyon, bottom right, riding to Westminster Abbey to become Duchess of York. Above, the official wedding portrait: HRH Prince Albert, Duke of York, and his bride, 26 April 1923 – the Duchess in her wedding dress by Madame Handley Seymour. Middle right, the couple on their honeymoon. Top left and right, two postcards published in 1923. Far right, Elizabeth, Duchess of York, in August 1925, a birthday portrait by Philip de Lazlo.

*E*lizabeth Bowes Lyon – an engagement
portrait, January 1923. Right, a
study by the society photographer Van Dyk.

*E*lizabeth, Duchess of York, in 1928. Pinned
to her dress is the family order of her father-
in-law, King George V. Right, a portrait painted
by Savely Sorine in 1923, the year of her
engagement and marriage.

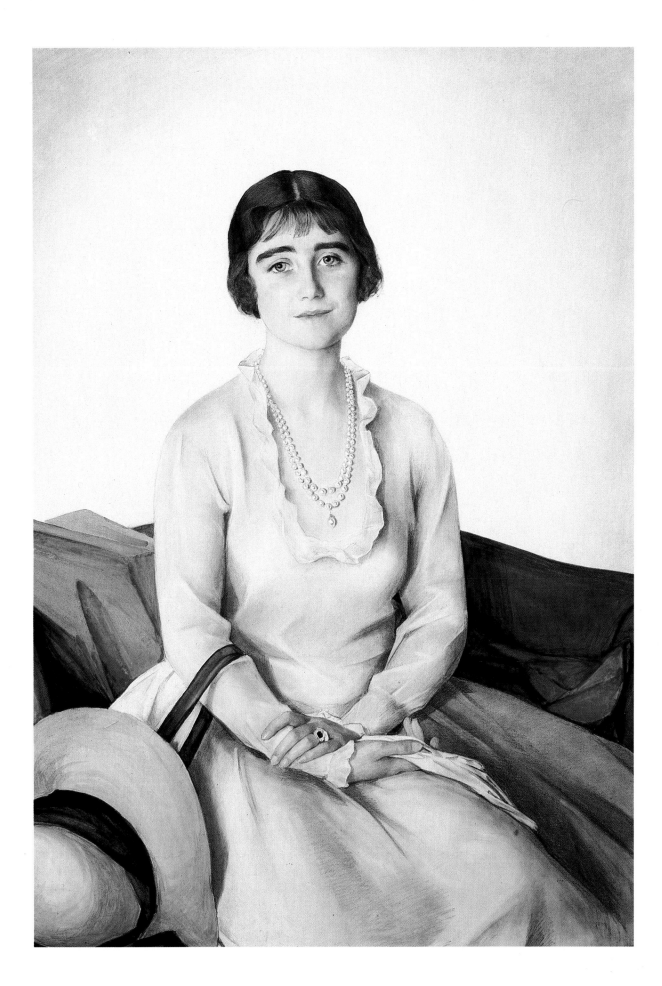

*D*ressed for the occasion. The Duchess of York in high 20's fashions for a fund-raising ceremony at Studley College, Warwickshire, July 1929. Right, salmon fishing during a tour of New Zealand, 1927. Far right, an early colour photograph by Bertram Park, July 1931.

Bertram Park

*F*amily portraits. The Duke and Duchess of
York with their 14-month-old daughter,
Princess Elizabeth, top, and, below, with proud
grandparents – King George V and Queen Mary
(left), the Earl and Countess of Strathmore (right),
June 1927. Right, 'Mother and Child', a hand-
tinted study by Marcus Adams.

R *ole models. The Duchess of York with her*
daughters, the Princesses Elizabeth and
Margaret Rose. Right, at Royal Lodge, Windsor, in
June 1936, six months before the Abdication.

God Bless Them!

Queen Elizabeth on Coronation Day with her Maids of Honour – her dress by Handley Seymour, theirs by Norman Hartnell. Below, a souvenir postcard, with a commemorative Coronation coin. Right, a new Royal Family.

PORTRAITS BY DOROTHY WILDING

DOROTHY WILDING

*I*conography. Dorothy Wilding, a leading society
photographer, was commissioned early in 1937 to
photograph Queen Elizabeth, above and left, and King George
VI, left, for the new stamps issued following their accession. The
diamond fringe tiara worn by Queen Elizabeth is a royal
heirloom dating back to Hanoverian times. It was worn
previously by her mother-in-law, Queen Mary, and later by her
daughter, Princess Elizabeth, on her wedding day in 1947.

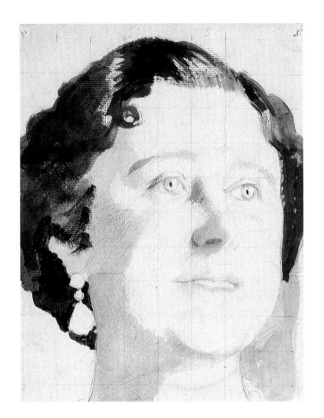

*S*tate portraits are, by tradition, commissioned on
the accession of a new sovereign, to be copied and
hung in British embassies and government houses
around the world. Gerald Kelly – 'the most reliable
portrait painter of his time', according to Sir Kenneth
Clark – started his sketches of Queen Elizabeth (above)
in October 1938, and got his friend, Sir Edwin
Lutyens, to provide the background, a small scale model
of Viceroy's House, the palace which Lutyens had
designed in Delhi. Although Kelly experimented, above
right, with an unfinished portrait of Queen Elizabeth
in one of Hartnell's 'Winterhalter' gowns, the vast
State Portrait itself, right, nearly 9 feet high and 6
feet wide, showed the Queen in her Coronation gown
by Handley Seymour. Kelly, a perfectionist who rubbed
out and repainted his work time after time, contrived to
become a semi-permanent guest at Windsor Castle
during the Second World War, not completing the state
portraits until 1945. When George VI knighted the
artist in that year for his efforts on the portraits and
other paintings, the band struck up 'Has anybody here
seen Kelly?'

The Winterhalter Queen

*C*hic, but not royal. Norman Hartnell's daywear designs for Queen Elizabeth before the Second World War. The classic Queen Elizabeth look had not yet evolved. Below, the little princesses, Margaret Rose and Elizabeth (behind her mother), leaving the Hartnell salon at 26 Bruton Street after a fitting for bridesmaids' dresses.

*R*oyal style. Top, Franz Xaver Winterhalter's portraits of the
Empress Elizabeth of Austria (upper left), and of Queen Victoria.
King George VI 'made it clear,' Norman Hartnell later recalled, 'that I
should attempt to capture this picturesque grace in the dresses I was to
design for the Queen.' Above, Hartnell's design for the dress worn by
Queen Elizabeth to the Bagatelle garden party in Paris, July 1938.
Right, a Hartnell outfit from the same wardrobe photographed in the
garden of Buckingham Palace by Cecil Beaton, July 1939.

*W*ith the minimum of effort the mouth forms a
smile which is as fresh as a dewdrop . . .
*Her dark hair seems to belong to another more
conventional and adult woman. The appearance
combines that of a child and a great lady . . . How
could I fail to make entrancing pictures?'*

Cecil Beaton on his July 1939 photo session with Queen Elizabeth at
Buckingham Palace

*T*he Queen watched her reflection in the long looking-glasses and was pleased with
the various effects, like a pretty child in a new party dress. Then the sun shone for
the first time this day to give me new inspiration. We took many more pictures with shafts
of light pouring down from the high windows on the small figure that stood in the
distance looking like an illustration to a fairy story.'

Cecil Beaton, Buckingham Palace, July 1939

*O*n tour. Queen Elizabeth in Paris, top, at the afternoon party in the garden of the Bagatelle, July 1937. Centre, embarking for Canada and the US, May 1939. Bottom, with Mrs Eleanor Roosevelt in Washington, June 1939. Right, back home again, in front of the Waterloo Urn, Buckingham Palace, July 1939.

'Through all the horror shone such courage and hope and trust'

King George VI and Queen Elizabeth after the bombing of Buckingham Palace, 10 September 1940.

I can look the East End in the face.' Top, Queen
Elizabeth tours bomb damage in south London,
September 1940. Below, a visit to Bath in 1942. Right, in
the deep shelters, London, November 1940.

*U*nfinished portrait. Augustus John, an extremely shy and nervous man,
had several sittings for this portrait with Queen Elizabeth in the early
months of the Second World War. Sherry was introduced into the sittings,
and a bottle of brandy discreetly left in the painter's equipment cupboard at
the Palace in the hope of calming the artist's nerves – but he abandoned the
project: only the sketch, above, appeared (published in 'Vogue' in 1941).
Then, twenty years later, the painting itself (right) was discovered in John's
cellar, covered with dust and cobwebs, in a pile of other canvases. It was
presented to the Queen Mother, who hung it over the fireplace of her
drawing-room at Clarence House, where it hangs to this day. 'I want to tell
you what a tremendous pleasure it gives me to see it once again,' she wrote to
John on 19 July 1961. 'It looks so lovely in my drawing-room and has
cheered it up no end! The sequins glitter and the roses and the red chair give
a fine glow, and I am so happy to have it . . .'

*T*hey will not leave me. I will not leave
the King – and the King will never
leave.' Two studies from a photo session in
July 1941 showing the Queen and her
daughters 'somewhere in the country'.

*Q*ueen Elizabeth and her daughters.
Two wartime studies by Cecil Beaton,
October 1942.

*V*ictory. The Royal Family on the balcony of Buckingham Palace,
with Winston Churchill, VE Day, 8 May 1945. Top, Queen
Elizabeth greets repatriated prisoners of war at a Buckingham Palace
garden party in May 1945. Facing page, scenes from a wartime life.

'A sort of peace...'

*T*he Royal Family in the garden at Royal Lodge, Windsor, July
1946. Right, a portrait by Sir James Gunn, 1945–6. Queen
Elizabeth, 45, wears one of her favourite pieces of jewellery, Queen
Victoria's diamond tassel brooch, also worn by Queen Alexandra.

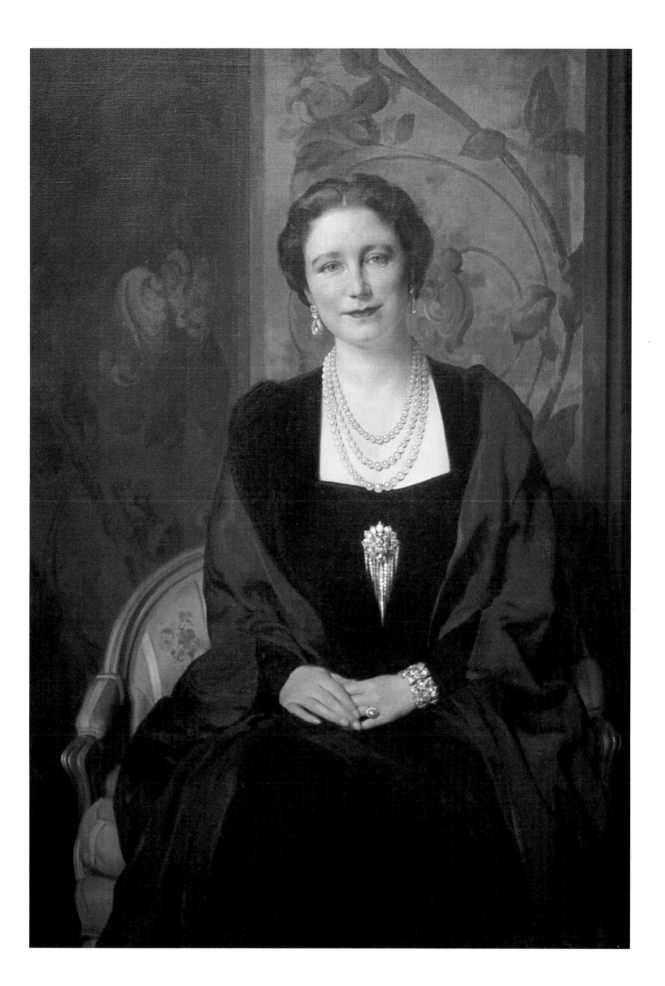

*S*ilver Wedding, 26 April 1948. Right, 'Conversation Piece' at Royal Lodge, Windsor, by Sir James Gunn, 1950, completed two years before the death of King George VI. The Queen Mother has had this room, the saloon at Royal Lodge, regularly redecorated, but always in the identical shade of green. Inset right, Gunn's working sketch, which now hangs in Clarence House.

*F*arewell. King George VI waves goodbye to his
   daughter, Princess Elizabeth, as she leaves for East
Africa, 31 January 1952. Top, at his final Royal
Command Performance. Right, three Queens.

Daily Mirror

TUES
FEB. 12
1952

FORWARD WITH THE PEOPLE

1½d

No. 15,007

Registered at G.P.O.
as a Newspaper.

A sorrowing family group of three Queens——Elizabeth the Second, Queen Mary and the Queen Mother——stand at the entrance to Westminster Hall as the King's coffin is carried past them to the Lying-in-State. On the right is Princess Margaret.

'*We could not possibly do without Mummy*'

*T*he Queen Mother, Coronation Day,
2 June 1953, with her grandchildren, Prince Charles and Princess Anne,
photographed by Cecil Beaton.

A new life. Time off for fishing during a tour
of New Zealand, 1966. Right, with her
grandchildren, 1954, and outside the Castle of
Mey, Caithness, in 1955 at the end of three years'
rebuilding and renovation.

*T*hirty years on. Cecil Beaton spent another summer's afternoon with his favourite royal subject in 1970, when she was 69 (and he was 66). Previous page, the terrace at Royal Lodge, Windsor. Above, the Queen Mother at the door to her study, and, right, among the rhododendrons. Inset, Beaton's watercolour commemorating the occasion.

A day at the races. The Queen Mother studies the form. Above right,
with one of her steeplechasers – note the light blue raincoat. Susan
Crawford's painting of the Queen Mother with the stallion, Bustino, a
leading sire at the Royal Studs, was sold in aid of the Injured Jockeys' Fund.
Overleaf, the Queen Mother presents the shamrock to the Irish Guards,
St Patrick's Day, 1987.

BUSTINO

*T aking Grandma for a spin. Every Easter David
Linley, son of Princess Margaret and Lord Snowdon,
has taken his grandmother over to see friends at Adelaide
Cottage, Windsor — by Mini, MGB and father's old
Aston. Overleaf, chocolate time. Queen Mother and
daughter at Birkhall, Balmoral, with five good boys.*

Ladies' Day. Spring 1980.
Made by Rudolf in the year that he died.

Sunny Days. Summer 1982.
Made for the christening of Prince William.

Spectator. Summer 1982.
At the Chelsea Flower Show.

Favourite. Spring 1983.
The brooch, a wedding present from Bertie.

*I*n 1969 Norman Hartnell introduced the Queen Mother to the milliner Rudolf (Zdenko Rudolf von Ehrenfeld, an exiled Czech nobleman), and she has worn Rudolf hats ever since. Each hat is designed in conjunction with a specific Hartnell outfit, and each hat has a name — the Queen Mother sometimes suggesting themes like 'Bersagliere' (prompted by memories of a childhood visit to Florence). You never see her holding on to her hat because each creation is, in a way, two hats. Underneath is a cloche-like bandeau which fits closely over her bun at the back. The actual hat is then mounted on to this. Since Rudolf's death in 1980, his work has been carried on by his partner, Joy Quested-Nowell, who now only makes hats for Queen Elizabeth the Queen Mother.

Investiture. *July 1977.*
To attend the knighting of Norman Hartnell.

Cavalier. *Autumn 1976.*
Her country hat.

Bersagliere. *Autumn 1985.*
'I'd love a Bersagliere!'

Springtime. *1974.*
Old faithful.

Shooting Hat. *No date.*
When one wears out she gets another.

Gold Cup. *Spring 1983.*
Worn with Queen Victoria's Jubilee brooch.

Rare Pearl. *Spring 1977.*
A favourite, designed by Rudolf.

Spring Meeting. *Spring 1986.*
To attend the Cheltenham races.

Sunny Days *(again). Summer 1982.*
The lilac straw version.

Encore. *Autumn 1976.*
'We keep on repeating it.'

Derby Day. *Spring 1984.*
Pistachio for the big day.

Imperial. *Summer 1986.*
An 86th birthday treat.

*M*atriarch. With her daughters,
photographed by Norman Parkinson on
her 80th birthday. Right, with her youngest great-
grandson, Prince Harry, December 1984,
photographed by Snowdon.

*N*ew recruits. The Queen Mother at Ascot in
1986 with the Princess of Wales – and
another Duchess of York.

*T*he years telescope. Birthday celebrations outside Clarence House, 4 August 1986, above and lower right. Standing in the doorway behind and to the right of the Queen Mother, her Private Secretary, Sir Martin Gilliat. Upper right, Grocer Philip Delaney outside the general store, Prestbury, Gloucestershire.

*A*t home. Queen Elizabeth the Queen
Mother at Clarence House, 2nd June
1987, photographed by Snowdon.

*O*n duty, at ease. Queen Elizabeth the Queen
Mother, in Clarence House, and at the
Finnish Hut, Balmoral, August 1983.

Queen Mother

◆

ecil Beaton first met Queen Elizabeth one July morning shortly after she and George VI had returned from North America in the summer of 1939. The photographer had expected to be entranced, and he was not disappointed: 'Before my eyes swam a hazy impression of a room with blue silk walls embroidered with bouquets of silver and white flowers. Flower pictures in gold frames, and real flowers everywhere – hydrangeas, sweet peas, carnations. The Queen, in pale grey, looked dazzlingly pink and white in the glaring light from the huge garden windows.'

Beaton could see his photograph already. He had been summoned for a portrait session with the Queen that afternoon, and Her Majesty had some ideas about what she might be wearing.

'I thought – perhaps – I might wear – a *dress* which perhaps you *know* – with bead embroideries? Perhaps you know I wore it – in *Canada*?' Beaton noticed how, at the end of every sentence, the royal voice trailed upwards, gently, in interrogation. 'And then – perhaps a dress of *tulle*, do you think? And a – ' (and this she said with a wistful air of apology) 'A – *tiara*?'

It takes one showman to appreciate another. Beaton asked that Her Majesty should wear as much jewellery as possible. 'The choice isn't very great, you know,' replied the Queen in a remark which might have been a gentle royal joke, or might have referred to the fact that, after the death of George V, Queen Mary had hung on to vast amounts of royal jewellery for herself.

Explaining that he was planning to use very strong photographic lamps that afternoon, Beaton asked if, perhaps, Her Majesty might attempt a strong make-up.

'I'll try, if you really need it,' she replied, 'but I'm not very good at it, you know.'

One of Cecil Beaton's trademarks had become the use of whimsical backgrounds culled from classical paintings – trees by Fragonard, a ruined arch by Piranesi. He photographically enlarged these into huge backdrops eight or more feet high, so that, with the addition of real chairs, flowers, statues and lighting, he could place his subject in what effectively became a theatrical set. It was in such a set, in the Yellow Drawing Room at Buckingham Palace, surrounded by massed banks of flowers from Windsor Castle, that he started to photograph Queen Elizabeth in July 1939.

Beaton had feared that his strong floodlights might destroy the fragility of his subject – strange how a lady of such stalwart construction should quite often evoke similar fears – but when the lights went on, the Queen looked even more radiant:

The arms and wrists are white and rounded as those of an early Victorian marble statue; the hands are country hands, rather than those of someone living in a city, with the fingernails cut short and mercifully without varnish; her dark hair seems to belong to another, more conventional and adult woman; the appearance combines that of a child and a great lady.

The session moved from the Yellow Drawing Room to the Blue, through various other settings in the State Apartments and then, eventually, out into the Palace gardens, where the Queen was most amused to find Beaton angling her round so that he shot with the light coming from behind her, almost directly into the lens. 'We always have to spend our time running round to face the sun,' she said, 'for the King's snapshots.'

The Queen had changed several times in the course of the afternoon, and now she was wearing a white, cobweb-lace dress, with parasol, like the outfit which had been such a sensation at the Bagatelle garden party in Paris. The session with Beaton, scheduled only to last half an hour or so, had extended through the whole afternoon, and by this time it was past six o'clock, with the evening sunlight slanting in fitful splashes through the trees. The atmosphere was 'strange and timeless', thought Beaton as he moved around in circles, snapping with his camera while the Queen made her way towards the lake.

Dusk compelled him finally to surrender his subject to the cars waiting to take her down to Windsor for the weekend. 'I can't bear to say goodbye,' the photographer confessed. But he did leave the Palace with one souvenir. While in the Yellow Drawing Room, the Queen had tucked her pocket handkerchief behind the cushion of a chair, and when she was not looking, Beaton lost no time in scampering to retrieve it and to bear it home in triumph, still scented with her perfume of gardenias and tuberoses.

Cecil Beaton was a romantic, and a snob. He was to enjoy his greatest popular success with the costumes he designed for the stage and film versions of *My Fair Lady* – the story of an ordinary woman transformed into something different. His middle-class background and his homosexuality gave him much in common with Norman Hartnell: both men had it, that sharp, aspiring outsider's eye for what delineates class, the drive to glamorize their own lives by lending glamour to those of others. In 1937 Hartnell had defined the mixture of the magical and mundane which was the new Queen Elizabeth. Now, two years later, Cecil Beaton captured this same compelling ambivalence and etched it permanently into the soft greys of his silver nitrate plate. Not surprisingly, perhaps, the two men did not get on particularly well, but they viewed each other's work with wary respect. In July 1939 the Queen told Beaton that Hartnell had spotted him in the Palace and had been very intrigued because, she twinkled, 'I expect he had visions of his lovely dresses appearing again.'

Cecil Beaton's 1939 photographs of Queen Elizabeth completed the process which made her a national emblem. They were at the time, and remain even today, despite their familiarity, quite breathtaking. They stand as the definitive royal photographs. There is a radiance about them, a mist of secret gardens and past glories and fairy tales which can almost be sniffed. The Queen is Gloriana, Titania, Britannia, a blend of evocations no less effective for being so obviously contrived, since Beaton's artifice, like all the best artifice, has the charm to suspend disbelief – a disarming quality shared, of course, in no small measure, by the lady herself.

By the time the pictures were published in December 1939, war with Germany had been declared. 'Taken in all the full regalia, they are very grand and do not look like wartime pictures,' worried Beaton. But for that very reason, the photographs were an immense success. Every single national newspaper published them, as did *The Lady*, *Country Life*, and almost all the illustrated magazines. 'Pictures that the people of Britain will treasure,' announced the *Daily Sketch*. In America *Life* ran one of the photographs on its cover.

That month, the photograph of the Queen in her tiara was used on a Christmas card which was sent in the name of the King and Queen to every man and woman serving in the armed forces. 'May God bless you and protect you, Elizabeth R George RI.' It was pinned up beside bunks, in billets and mess rooms. It was stowed in the kitbags of men crossing the Channel to fight in France. It became a universal image, soft and yielding, something to be cherished and protected, a few square inches of card which summed up the gentleness and refinement that Britain was fighting for – 'a continuing inspiration to the Empire in the Fight against Nazi-ism,' as the *Illustrated London News* described her. Through Cecil Beaton's adoring, fanciful photograph, Queen Elizabeth had become a modern talisman – a battle favour that fluttered bravely on the modern jouster's lance.

———————◆———————

One day in the summer of 1940, when the Battle of Britain was at its height, Harold Nicolson, now working in the Ministry of Information, went to lunch at Buckingham Palace. The year had seen a succession of catastrophes – the surrender of Belgium, the fall of France, the seemingly inexorable advance of the German armies, who now stood on the other side of the Channel, waiting their moment to cross. Nicolson felt demoralized, under strain. The terrible emergency was keeping him up in town, night after night, away from his beloved Sissinghurst, and he confided to the Queen how he sometimes got homesick.

'But that is right,' she said. 'That is personal patriotism. That is what keeps us going. I should die if I had to leave.'

She told Nicolson that she was taking revolver lessons every morning. 'I shall not go down like the others,' she said – the others, presumably, being the assorted European royal relatives who had pitched up in London with their suitcases, and had turned Buckingham Palace into something of a rooming house.

'I cannot tell you how superb she was,' wrote Nicolson that night to his wife, Vita Sackville-West.

Nicolson was also impressed by the transformation that kingship and a creative wife had wrought in George VI, whom he had once thought of as 'rather a foolish loutish boy'. The King had, somehow, taken on some of the lightness and charm of his elder brother, the Duke of Windsor – and the diarist walked out of the Palace feeling elated.

'He was so gay and she was so calm,' he told his wife. 'They did me all the good in the world... WE SHALL WIN. I know that. I have no doubts at all.'

'They will not leave me. I will not leave the King – and the King will never leave.' These famous words of Queen Elizabeth in response to the suggestion, in the darkest days of the Second World War, that she might send her daughters out of the country for safekeeping, have often been repeated. Their context is the revolver practice on the Palace lawn. It is like her response to the bombing of Buckingham Palace in September 1940: 'I'm glad we've been bombed. It makes me feel I can look the East End in the face.' It loses some of its impact when you know that we won – and especially if you were not bombed yourself. King George VI, in fact, was furious about the bombing of his home. He took it very personally, complaining – without any evidence, so far as is known – that one of his relatives in the German air force had been piloting the plane and had done it quite deliberately.

During the First World War, King George V and Queen Mary had set an example to the nation by forswearing alcohol for the duration. Buckingham Palace went dry. King George VI and his wife did not make the same mistake. But they set a conscientious example in all other respects, particularly when it came to food rationing. The Dowager Viscountess Hambleden, a lady-in-waiting then as now, remembers taking her own stock of biscuits with her whenever she went on a tour of duty on the royal train. 'Really, I was quite hungry.'

Eleanor Roosevelt, returning the royal visit of 1939, was less disturbed by the quantity than by the quality of Palace fare. Turnip jam and reconstituted egg powder were staples – 'probably sawdust,' admitted Her Majesty quite happily.

Mrs Roosevelt also missed American central heating. She was lent the Queen's bedroom and froze in it, draughts whistling through the makeshift windows patched up with wooden frames and mica.

Quite early in the war Norman Hartnell was summoned to discuss the Queen's costume for the hostilities. It was comparatively easy to stick to the government rules for 'austerity' dressing – a limited number of seams per dress, narrow collars and belts, a minimum of frills. Embroidery was forbidden, so Hartnell hand-painted garlands of lilac on one white satin gown which, with jewels, became the Queen's standard uniform at diplomatic soirées. The more difficult question was what should be worn for visiting bombed sites and disaster areas. Black or sombre colours, standard royal wear for visits of sympathy in peace time, did not, somehow, seem appropriate now. There was a need for a little optimism, a hint of the light at the end of the tunnel. Churchill managed it rather well with his siren suit and big cigar, which struck just the right note of hard work and jauntiness.

Since the Winterhalter inspiration, Hartnell's touch with Queen Elizabeth's formal State dress had been faultless. The Bruton Street crinoline had become the basis of her grand evening look, and it was, in fact, to remain the standard, full dress, ship-of-the-line silhouette for royal ladies until the advent of the new Princess of Wales in the early 1980s – the very embodiment of that inaccurate yet universally understood phrase 'the Queen of England'.

But by 1939 Hartnell still had not got the daywear right. Not realizing, perhaps, that the royal costume for visiting a factory or hospital required, in its way, the same theatrical unreality as a grand evening gown, he had designed contemporary daytime outfits for Queen Elizabeth in the late 1930s that were really no different from those he was preparing for his other wealthy clients. You could see them every teatime by the dozen at the Ritz. Looking for glamour in the wrong direction, he had also tried to camouflage the shape of his royal subject, vainly seeking to squeeze her into the sleek, angular wedge of an Evelyn Laye.

But then came the war, and when forced to contemplate the meaning of what a Queen should wear to a scene of disaster or wartime endeavour, Norman Hartnell stopped focusing on fashion. Being fashionable, in any case, was out of harmony with the wartime ethic. There were other priorities. The Queen had a job to do, and her clothes had to show it: she had to be instantly recognizable, her aura should be cheerful, and she should very obviously *not* be engaged upon a shopping trip to Mayfair. It did not matter if she looked homely – indeed, as it happened, that was rather to the point. Queen Elizabeth's very matronliness suddenly became of the essence.

Hartnell changed direction. He took his existing palate of royal colours – blue, pink and lilac, but excluding green, which some might consider unlucky –

and made them less strident. He then started designing his clothes around his client's shape – 'very sweet and *soignée*,' as Mrs Winston Churchill put it, 'like a plump turtle dove' – and thus was liberated the round, comfortable silhouette topped off with a hat that still stands for the Queen Mother: a touch of Women's Institute, a touch of Pearly Queen.

The firm little figure picking her way through rubble in high heels and muted pastel became one of the vignettes which encapsulated people's wartime experience. 'The Queen nips out into the snow and goes straight into the middle of the crowd and starts talking to them,' said Lord Harlech who accompanied her on one of her visits, this one to Sheffield in 1941. 'For a moment or two they just gaze and gape in astonishment. But then they all start talking at once. "Hi! Your Majesty, look here!"'

In London a woman was trying to coax her terrified dog to come out from under a pile of rubble. 'Perhaps I can try,' asked the Queen. 'I am rather good with dogs.'

Not everyone was impressed with her visits, according to the volunteers of Mass Observation, the organization which tried to keep a finger on the pulse of grass roots Britain through a haphazard system of interviews and eavesdroppings. 'I suppose they do a certain amount of good coming round, but I wish they would give me a new house,' was one Southampton woman's view of the King and Queen in December 1940. This unromantic sort of comment did not command much public circulation at the time, and has not been greatly favoured by Queen Elizabeth's biographers since. But its worn desperation oddly echoes a certain tone of her own, when speaking in private. Taking refuge in the Buckingham Palace bomb shelter with Roosevelt's envoy, Harry Hopkins, in January 1941, she confessed that she found it extremely difficult to put words to her feelings for the ordinary people of Britain. Writing to her mother-in-law, Queen Mary, she described how 'exhausted' she felt after having seen and heard such sadness and sorrow, along with all the heroism. 'The destruction is so awful, & the people so *wonderful* – they *deserve* a better world.'

In the spring of 1943 she wrote to Ava Anderson, wife of John Anderson, the Chancellor of the Exchequer, thanking her for the gift of a couple of books, one of them a book of French poetry, *Les Lilas et les Roses*, which she found 'very touching and poignant':

I think it is odd that *our* poets were dumb at that glorious moment when the British Isles stood against the oppressor, it is disappointing that they do not seem to see the significance of our crusade against slavery and lies – do you not agree? I know that the cruelty & the ugliness & bestiality of the bombing in 1940 must have been difficult to write about, but through all the horror shone such courage & hope & trust.

Handwritten like all her thank-you letters, it was spontaneous and not particularly thought out. But, like all her letters, it betrayed strong emotion – a feeling, caring, rather old-fashioned response which came from her rather old-fashioned roots. During the First World War the Strathmore family set up a hospital in their ancestral home at Glamis, and the teenage Elizabeth worked there as a nurse, generating deep affection among the wounded soldiers that she cared for. It was not done to catch the eye of cameras or reporters. It only became known of later when the Earl's daughter became a national figure. It was done because that was what you did – duty, commitment, *noblesse oblige*. The strength of Queen Elizabeth came from this bedrock feeling, and also from a strain of thoughtfulness that ran deeper than her unfailing smile might suggest.

'You mustn't be serious, my dear one,' says Elyot, in Noel Coward's *Private Lives*, an extract from which the Queen Mother chose as a favourite scene for her eighty-fifth birthday radio programme in August 1985. 'It's just what they want.'

'Who's they?' asks Amanda.

'All the futile moralists who try to make life unbearable. Laugh at them. Be flippant. Laugh at everything – all their sacred shibboleths. Flippancy brings out the acid in all their damned sweetness and light.'

Penelope Mortimer quotes this scene at the conclusion of her acute yet vinegary biography of the Queen Mother as indicating the theatricality of the lady – and hence her superficiality as well. But the cheeriness being advocated by Elyot and by Noel Coward is not hollow. It is based on an all-too-aching awareness of pain, which must be wrapped up and carried bravely forward, not brooded over.

Wearing pink to the bombed site did not preclude caring. On the contrary. Asked many years later how she felt when the war was finally over, Queen Elizabeth replied, 'We felt absolutely *whacked*.'

either King George VI nor Queen Elizabeth could be numbered among nature's socialists. The two of them might, in an earlier age, have been classified as Whig, since their conservatism did not exclude genuine social concern. But they were scarcely soulmates of the Labour government which swept into power at the end of the Second World War in a flurry of nationalization and empire destruction – and for this very reason, perhaps, the post-war social gatherings at which the King and Queen entertained their Cabinet ministers took on a fun and boisterousness which they had not known before.

They were known as 'dine-and-sleeps', since the invitation was for dinner at Windsor and a night in the castle, with a fairly prompt and non-ceremonial departure expected before lunch next day. The guests, which now included a fair sprinkling of trades union leaders, the new establishment, arrived in time for drinks with the King and Queen. They then retired to change for dinner. Sir Stafford Cripps, the unbending Labour Chancellor of the Exchequer, starchily insisted on vegetarian dishes which, somehow, always looked better than the food that everyone else was eating. Ladies and gentlemen went their separate ways after dinner, but if the men lingered longer than half an hour over their port and cigars, they could expect the arrival of a footman with a polite little note from the Queen.

It was then that the jollity started. During the war George VI had several times had to review the Free Polish troops stationed in Britain, taking the marchpast as they did the 'Parada', a high, stiff, leg-kicking walk not that different from the Nazi goose-step. The King and Queen were most amused.

'Oh, Bertie,' said the Queen one dine-and-sleep evening at Windsor, 'let's do the *Parada*!'

So the King took his station by the fireplace, stiffly to attention, the gramophone was switched on, and to the scratchy tones of a military march, the assembled Cabinet ministers and members of the household goose-stepped past him, eyes left, the Chancellor of the Exchequer putting on a particularly good show, upright as ever, with a pair of fire tongs on his shoulder instead of a rifle.

It was growing up at Glamis that Elizabeth Bowes Lyon had learned how to get a party going. The Strathmores would gather round the piano after dinner with their guests for a sing-song and silly games. It helped loosen the atmosphere at Windsor no end. Even Queen Mary would enter into the spirit of things, sticking a matchbox on her nose then nuzzling up to the gentleman next to her to pass it onwards. There was 'Racing Demon', a complicated version of patience at which Princess Margaret has been world champion for forty years, charades – and even 'Murder'. Appointed detective for one game and groping in the darkness beneath a piano, Ben Nicolson, Deputy Surveyor of the King's Pictures in the mid-1940s, poked his finger into what he thought was a soft cushion, to discover he had located the Queen.

The evening might conclude with a conga, led vigorously up and down staircases by a member of the royal family, after which the guests would line up formally to wish Their Majesties good night. George VI and Queen Elizabeth would then take their leave through a pair of high double doors which were formally closed behind them – except that on one occasion the catch slipped, and before the door could be closed again, the assembled guests caught a glimpse of the King and Queen, on their own, skipping down the corridor, hand in hand, towards their private apartments.

n February 1947, the journalist James Cameron found himself covering the visit of King George VI and Queen Elizabeth to South Africa. This rather surprised him, since he disliked both royalty and South Africa. Then, equally to his surprise, he found the trip quite fun.

'No two personalities could have been more different than those of the King and Queen,' he wrote. Travelling with other journalists in the same train as George VI and Queen Elizabeth, Cameron saw them both at first hand every day. 'She was, then as now,' he later wrote in the *Guardian*, 'composed, eager, on top of every situation; he was tense, unbearably nervous, alternating diffidence with sharp bursts of temper.'

The object of the tour was to foster goodwill between the nations of what was becoming known as the Imperial Commonwealth, and, in particular, to counteract the anti-British sentiments of the local Afrikaans community. *Ex Unitate Vires* – 'From Unity, Strength,' read the South African motto on the tablecloth in the royal dining car. 'Huh!' exclaimed the King when he first set eyes upon it. 'Not much bloody *Unitate* about this place!'

The King's mind seemed fixed on Britain, where an appalling cold spell was complicating a life already grim with ration books and nationalized austerity. 'He kept saying he should be at home and not lolling about in the summer sun,' wrote Cameron. 'Never was a man so jumpy. The Queen kept smiling through.'

Three or four times a day the royal train – somewhat insensitively named the White Train – would draw to a halt for a visit. The King would stand by the door lingeringly, not wanting very much to descend. But then, wrote Cameron, 'the Queen would appear beside him, looking (the word is inescapable) radiant, or at any rate full of beans.

'"Oh, Bertie, do you see, this is Hicksdorp! You know we've always so wanted to see Hicksdorp! Those people there with the bouquets – they must be the local councillors. *How* kind! And those people at the far, far end of the platform, behind that little fence – I expect they are the Bantu choir. How kind! We must wave, Bertie."'

And so the King found himself nudged into action. One stop was at Outshoorn, a centre of the ostrich feather trade, where George VI was scheduled to nip a tail-feather off an ostrich. Understandably more nervous than usual, the King fumbled with his clippers, nicking a quarter of an inch off the ostrich's backside, at which the captive and offended creature let forth an indignant squawk.

'Enter the Queen, stage right, as usual in total smiling command. She took the clippers from her husband, and there and then did an absolutely expert featherectomy – snip.'

She turned and spoke to the nearest bystander, who happened to be James Cameron.

'We do a lot of gardening at home...' she explained. 'The King is good at the digging and the weeding. It is I who concentrate on the secateurs.'

◆

The Household blamed the royal 'gnashes' on the war. The King had gone through so much. It had stripped his nerves. For a man who had barely turned fifty, George VI really looked quite old. He was drawn and taut. The hope had been that South Africa – the warmth, the long cruise there and back – might prove a turning point.

It was when he got back, however, that he really started to sicken. People did not take it in, what with all the excitement of his elder daughter's marriage to Prince Philip at the end of 1947, but the King kept on losing weight. At the end of a day's shooting at Balmoral he would call his private secretaries into his study for half an hour or so, and they noticed that he would be rubbing his legs. He said that they felt cold.

By the autumn of 1948 he was in the hands of the doctors. They operated the following spring, but still, when he went shooting he needed electrically heated suits and gloves. He found it difficult to shake off colds and 'flu. He was starting to cough a lot.

When he went back to the surgeons in the autumn of 1951 it was for lung cancer. As he left Balmoral that year he had seemed to look around the place longer and harder than he usually did, searching out people to say goodbye. Lilibet and Philip were in East Africa, representing him on a tour that he had been scheduled to make himself, when he died in his sleep at Sandringham, some time in the small hours of 6 February 1952.

There was so much to do when his widow was woken with the news – the new Queen and her husband to be brought back home, the funeral to think of, telegrams to send.

'Poor lady,' said Kemp, one of her pages, remembering all the bustle of those days. 'She never had time to cry.'

◆

It was a cruel, early deprivation. They had celebrated their Silver Wedding a few years before he died, they were grandparents. But they had never, really, had a proper run at anything – pitchforked into Buckingham Palace, rushing through those pre-war tours, and then coping with the war. Bertie's funeral and the mourning in February 1952 stirred up the old bitterness about the abdication, and which of the brothers had the lines under his eyes.

But which of the brothers, as it turned out, had proved the greater man? Bertie might have lived longer if he had remained nothing more than Duke of

York, shooting and stalking to his heart's content, opening the odd hospital on the side. But had not the challenge of the throne drawn something extra from within the man – elevated him to a higher plane? The quality of a life is not measured by its duration. Bertie had taken his place among the kings.

Some time after the funeral, old Princess Marie Louise, Queen Victoria's grand-daughter, complimented the widowed Queen Elizabeth on the fortitude with which she was bearing her loss. She was putting such a brave face on things.

'Not in private,' the widow quietly replied.

She went back to the woods where Bertie had proposed to her, in the grounds of the Bowes Lyon home at St Paul's Walden Bury. She kept a little sitting room at Glamis as a sort of shrine, its photos and mementoes all dating from the first, happy years of their marriage. 'One cannot yet believe that it has all happened,' she wrote in one letter. 'One feels rather dazed.'

There are several theories as to what coaxed her out of the darkness. Winston Churchill went for a long, serious talk with her at Balmoral, speaking of duty and joy, it is thought. Then there was the sad, abandoned home she found in the very northeast tip of Scotland, the Castle of Mey, which she resolved to purchase and bring back to life, a parable for the rebuilding she now had to do alone.

'What happens if one of us dies?' asks Amanda. 'Does the one that's left still laugh?'

'Yes,' Elyot tells her, 'yes, with all his might... Death's very laughable, such a cunning little mystery. All done with mirrors.'

In the autumn of 1952, six months after Bertie's death, she went up to Scotland on her own. The artistic Sitwells had long been friends of hers – Osbert and Edith in particular. Their taste had a fey, aristocratic quality that struck a chord, and she took up to Scotland *A Book of Flowers*, an anthology of poems which Edith Sitwell had compiled, and had sent her as a gift.

It is giving me the greatest pleasure, [she wrote to Edith on 15 September 1952] and I took it out with me, and I started to read it, sitting by the river, and it was a day when one felt engulfed by great black clouds of unhappiness and misery, and I felt a sort of peace stealing round my heart as I read such lovely poems and heavenly words.

I found a hope in George Herbert's poem, 'Who could have thought my shrivel'd heart could have recovered greenesse? It was gone quite underground' and I thought how small and selfish sorrow is. But it bangs one about until one is senseless, and I can never thank you enough for giving me such a delicious book wherein I found so much beauty and hope, quite suddenly one day by the river.

t is May 1986, and Queen Elizabeth the Queen Mother is visiting Florence. This is not an official visit. She is wearing white leather shoes, a silk pastel suit and, yes, one of her hats. But she is here in a private capacity. She is a tourist, still sightseeing after all these years. You would have thought that the most senior member of the world's most travelled royal family – Queen Mother for more than thirty years, Queen for sixteen before that – would feel like a change. But, just coming up to her eighty-sixth birthday, Her Majesty Queen Elizabeth (her daughter, Queen Elizabeth II, is known as 'The Queen') loves few things more than 'looking around'.

Today she is visiting the Villa Capponi, a beautifully kept, sixteenth-century mansion owned by some Americans called Clifford, and she is enjoying herself immensely – sniffing the flowers, peeking round corners, pausing for long, absorbed minutes to drink in the pictures. She was last here seventy-five years ago, as a little girl of eleven. A relative of the Strathmores, Mrs Scott, lived in the Villa Capponi, decorously initiating young English ladies into the delights of the Italian Renaissance. To see the Queen Mother now, she could be a little girl again. For lunch it will be off to Marlia, near Lucca, then an afternoon enjoying the garden where Napoleon's sister used to stroll.

'Most people look exhausted at the end of a day's sightseeing – quite drained,' says Sir Harold Acton, the author and aesthete, who lives in a beautiful Tuscan villa of his own. 'But she draws strength from the experience. She *looks* with such enthusiasm and intelligence. She is giving of herself all the time.' Sir Harold, it hardly needs adding, worships unashamedly at her feet.

Queen Elizabeth the Queen Mother has been sightseeing in places like the Villa Capponi most months of May for more than twenty years now. It is her private pleasure, her ritual of spring. The Viscomte de Noailles invited her over to France in the early 1960s to stay in some congenial châteaux – among them Courances, the home of his relatives, the Ganay family – and a week of French leave grew into what is now an annual event. She has always liked to consider these trips as something of a secret: a few days off the record, sometimes in an hotel, more usually in the comfort of a (rather distinguished) private home.

But it is not quite that easy to stop being Queen Mother. One year, accompanied by Sir Pierson Dixon, then British ambassador to France, she requested an informal evening in a typical French bistro. Sir Pierson suggested there was a danger she might be recognized, but Her Majesty insisted that could not possibly be the case. So the ambassador had a tactful word with the local *préfet*, and on the evening of the royal visit, the small working-class French café was filled, wall-to-wall, with gendarmes and their wives, all dressed like ordinary French peasants, studiously taking no notice whatsoever of the cosy little English widow who turned up with her party of friends. She had a wonderful time. It only went to prove, she told the ambassador afterwards, how easy it was for her to go abroad, if she wanted, incognito.

oing private was always one option for her widowhood. Queen Victoria did it quite spectacularly, Queen Alexandra to a lesser degree. But for Queen Elizabeth the Queen Mother it was never a possibility. It involved a surrender of royalty that accorded neither with her tastes nor her beliefs. 'That is no age to give up your job,' sniffed Queen Mary on hearing that Queen Wilhelmina of the Netherlands, then sixty-eight, was planning to retire, and Queen Elizabeth the Queen Mother has always been of the same mind. Royalty is a job for life, a pleasure and a duty to be continued to the very end.

There was a suggestion, quite soon after the death of George VI, that she might be despatched for two or three years on a tour of duty to one of the dominions – Canada, perhaps, or Australia – as a Governor-General or some other form of semi-permanent royal ambassador. But Queen Elizabeth II would not hear of that.

'Oh no,' she said, 'we could not possibly do without Mummy.'

A more flexible option was royal touring – she had set the modern pattern of it, after all, in the late 1930s – and as Queen Mother it became a major part of her vocation: France twice (on official visits); the Federation of Rhodesia and Nyasaland twice; Australia, New Zealand and Fiji all twice; Kenya; Uganda; Italy; Gibraltar; Tunisia; Sardinia; Northern Ireland three times; Denmark; Iran; Cyprus; the Channel Islands; Holland; West Germany (to visit the British Army of the Rhine); Canada eight times – and the United States in 1954, the very first royal tour she carried out by herself. Broadway came to a standstill when the Queen Mother went to see *Pajama Game*. 'If she wasn't a Queen there's many a man who'd like to marry her,' remarked a New York cab driver caught in the traffic – adding, after further thought, 'She'd be a pleasing handful at playtime.'

There is only one real job in the British royal family. Elizabeth II does it. Prince Charles is waiting to do it – and every other member of the House of Windsor carves their own swathe. Queen Elizabeth the Queen Mother has been the matriarch since March 1953, when, just over a year after Bertie, old Queen Mary died. The image of a royal lady can go through a bumpy stage in middle life. The world has no difficulty idolizing glamorous princesses, or in venerating grand old ladies in their later years. It is the stage in between that can be tricky, when middle age incurs the risk of ordinariness.

Queen Elizabeth the Queen Mother escaped this almost entirely, skipping smartly, thanks to Queen Mary's considerate exit, from mother of the princesses to mother of the clan – and, by extension, to mother of the nation as a whole. Professor Sir Edmund Leach, the anthropologist, has remarked on the popular affection enjoyed by royal mother figures in modern Europe, pointing out that they have all flourished in cold, northern, Protestant countries who have decided they have no need of superstitious rituals like the veneration of the Mother of Christ.

But this is not an interpretation favoured by the lady herself, who takes religion – hers or anybody else's – very seriously, and who is also very conscious that, even if she has tucked Great Britain under her wing through the exercise of a certain charm, her majesty is ultimately a reflected glory.

'Do you realize, Ma'am,' asked a Labour politician at lunch with her one day, 'that if we set up a republic, everyone would want you to be the first president?'

'Oh, no,' replied Her Majesty, genuinely shocked by the idea. 'It would have to be the Queen.'

rance in May, Sandringham in July, August at the Castle of Mey, her restored home in the north of Scotland. The breaks have been dotted through her working schedule for more than a quarter of a century now. 'Having a routine,' explains her friend and lady-in-waiting, Lady Jean Rankin, 'is the only way to have any freedom.'

She goes to Sandringham in the summer so that she can visit the King's Lynn festival organized by Ruth, Lady Fermoy, another friend and lady-in-waiting, who is also grandmother to Lady Diana Spencer, now Princess of Wales. She goes to the concerts in the evening, and during the day she goes for walks and to visit the stallions and mares in the two adjacent royal studs.

'Why do you keep half of Mummy's mares at Sandringham and half over at Wolverton?' the Queen asked one day of Michael Oswald, who manages the studs in the two villages.

'Well, if I didn't, Ma'am,' Oswald replied, 'one groom would think that he hadn't had his fair share.'

'Yes,' said the Queen. 'That's the effect Mummy seems to have on people.'

Every July the Queen Mother is mistress of Sandringham again, just like the old days when Bertie was up there, shooting the duck at every opportunity he got. She loves the winds off the North Sea, the scent of salt in the air. She loves being outdoors generally – brisk, bracing walks with the dogs in almost any kind of weather. 'A good strong wind,' she says, 'blows the germs away.'

The germs seem to stay well clear of her, in any case. She is the most admirable advertisement for the royal family's faith in homeopathy. She has not had a drug in her body for more than fifty years, and she is gently crusading on behalf of homeopathy's natural way.

'I *must* have an aspirin!' says one of her attendants.

'An *aspirin?*' she says – managing to pronounce it as Lady Bracknell did 'handbag?' – '*Drugs?*'

She does not, in fact, greatly care to discuss medical matters. She grew up in an age when Princesses did not become pregnant. They simply 'ceased to undertake public engagements' after a particular date. Her doctors had the greatest difficulty even hinting at the complications attending the birth of her first daughter – 'a certain line of treatment was successfully adopted' – and as for the tummy trouble which landed her in hospital for a week or so in 1966, well, nobody discusses *that*.

She is not squeamish, however, about illness in others. The wife of one of her closest friends, Garrett, Lord Drogheda, has suffered from Alzheimer's disease for several years, and since it became serious Lord Drogheda has noticed that the Queen Mother has tended to drop in at their Windsor home more frequently, if anything, than she used to, whether he is there or not.

'She thinks that Joan still recognizes her, you see, even if she can't say so,' says a friend, 'and that visiting will bring her some comfort.'

Her sensitivity is most apparent in her letters. Her friends and relatives treasure them – two, four, six sides or more of her springy, elegant handwriting, with an inch wide margin down the left hand side: appreciative comments on a well-enjoyed lunch, support to a young relative whose marriage has gone wrong, some compassionate, rather moving thoughts on the death of a mutual friend who suffered from depression towards the end. She has the gift of intimacy when she writes, seeming to take your hand in hers for a page or so, before parting with a little twist of courtesy that is almost Jane Austen-like: 'Your loving g. aunt', 'I am your very affectionate friend, Elizabeth R' – with the big E at the one end and the big R at the other.

She spends a good hour or more working at her correspondence each morning. Thank-you letters go off next day, folded up, the envelope addressed and thoroughly licked, the whole process done properly by her, not handed to a lady-in-waiting to complete. She actually signs all her own Christmas cards – unlike the Queen and Prince Philip who have imitated political practice for some years now, and have recruited the help of an autopen. (Cognoscenti breathe moistly on their royal Christmas cards to tell if their signature came from the personal batch or the autopen – which betrays itself with a certain fuzziness.)

It all testifies to her extraordinary energy. 'What keeps her going?' asks one of her godchildren, who has the answer. 'Willpower. She simply does not admit that she is old.' People inviting her to dinner make a great mistake if they confine their guest list to the over-seventies. Three generations is the rule. She is not very keen on very small children, but once they are personalities in their own right she has the knack of treating them as equals, drawing on the experiences of her own childhood – the tedium of long journeys, say, in her case on the summer train up to Scotland: 'You know, once I made a banana last the *whole* way!'

When she is at Windsor she urges her house guests who have godchildren or grandchildren at Eton to invite them over for tea. Then she feeds the boys tea-cakes and cream and those cucumber sandwiches. 'Oh, *do* have another scone!'

She is best of all with her own grandchildren – warm and wise and supportive, a refuge: precisely what a grandmother should be. Princess Margaret's children found this at the time when their parents' marriage was breaking down. Prince Charles found it as a schoolboy, when he was wrestling with the hardships of Gordonstoun. Could she not, perhaps, persuade his parents to take him away from the place, he would ask when he met her at half-term? And she would say no to him, but gently, and promise that she would help him to face up to it – which she did. She knew a thing or two, after all, about putting backbone into kings.

'Ever since I can remember,' wrote Prince Charles in 1978, 'my grandmother has been the most wonderful example of fun, laughter, warmth, infinite security and above all else exquisite taste... For me she has always been one of those extraordinarily rare people whose touch can turn everything to gold.'

hilip Delaney first met the Queen Mother eighteen years ago. He had a grocer's shop at Leckhampton on the outskirts of Cheltenham, and the Queen Mother would drive past every year on her way to the races. One year Philip Delaney decided to organize a little party outside the shop, encouraging his customers to come and wave Union Jacks when the royal car came past at 4.30 p.m. – except that the car sped past early, at a quarter past four, before many of the celebrants had arrived. Great was the chagrin in Leckhampton that spring, and heavy the derision heaped upon Grocer Delaney.

'Why don't you find out the proper time next year, Philip?'

So Grocer Delaney decided to do just that, writing a letter to Clarence House to explain what had happened – and he received a reply not from some humble equerry, but from Sir Martin Gilliat himself, Private Secretary to Queen Elizabeth, saying how sorry Her Majesty had been to hear about the disappointment in Leckhampton.

Next year Philip Delaney gathered his customers outside his store with the firm assurance that the royal car would be going past at 4.30 p.m. precisely – except that the car did not go past. As Her Majesty saw the grocer standing in his white coat beside the road, she knocked on her chauffeur's partition, and the Daimler drew to a graceful halt.

In 1972 a sociological survey revealed that people's dreams about royalty would most commonly start with a parting of the parlour curtains to disclose a limousine drawing up outside – and here it was happening in Leckhampton. The Queen Mother opened her car door, and Philip Delaney, not unprepared for his dream coming true, stumbled forward to present Her Majesty with the bunch of flowers he had purchased that morning. He remembers them as being wild Cotswold daffodils gathered by a passing tinker – and if fairy godmothers can halt in the suburbs of Cheltenham in the late twentieth century, who is to doubt that wandering tinkers may not pass through also?

'Oh, Mr Delaney,' she said, as if she had known him all his life, 'are those flowers for *me?*'

'Yes, Ma'am' he said, proffering the daffodils. 'I'm sorry they are not roses or carnations.'

He passed the flowers across the front of the Queen Mother's travelling companion, the Duchess of Beaufort, and at that moment it became very clear that these were no flowers by Interflora, for a huge gobbet of slime off the unwashed stems dropped down from the bunch on to the Duchess's dress.

'I would *much* rather have these flowers than any carnations or roses,' declared the Queen Mother stoutly. 'I will see you next year.' And so she did, next year, and the year after that, and the year after that...

It is now 18 March 1987, and Philip Delaney is preparing for his eighteenth meeting with Her Majesty Queen Elizabeth – though they now meet before the races, and their rendezvous is no longer in Leckhampton. Mr Delaney had to give up the lease of his shop there in 1981, and when he got a job as manager of the general store in the not too distant village of Prestbury, the Queen Mother said that she should would like to keep on visiting him, even if it did involve a two or three mile detour.

This has made for more complex ceremonial, since Mr Delaney now has to introduce his new employer, Mr John Fogarty, to Her Majesty, along with Mr Fogarty's wife, Anne – and there has been one further embellishment, ever since the year that Mr Delaney supplemented his gift of flowers with a packet of peppermints.

QUEEN MOTHER

'Goodness,' she exclaimed, 'how *did* you know I like mints?'

'I read it somewhere,' said the grocer.

'Well, it's quite *true*,' said the Queen Mother. 'I wonder what you'll give me next year?'

So every year since Philip Delaney has scoured the sweet shops in search of a new sort of mint – crispy mints, champagne mints, chewy mints – even travelling up to London to enlist the help of the royal confectioners, Prestat. This year the flavour is ginger.

By 11.30, an hour before Queen Elizabeth's scheduled arrival, a small crowd has gathered outside the Prestbury General Store. Flags flutter loyally from the picturesque thatched roof.

'This is royal country,' says one spectator proudly. 'We've got Anne and Charles and Princess Michael living down the road.'

Another lady tells the story of how, one year, she was clipping her hedge, when she looked up to see the Queen Mother going past in her car. Her Majesty was just powdering her nose.

'She looked out and gave me such a lovely smile. I think we all feel better after seeing her.'

Mini-coaches and charabancs rumble past loaded with male parties of racegoers, flushed with British Rail breakfasts and the prospects of a good day out. Seeing the crowd and flags in the village high street, they throw themselves into exaggerated royal postures, giving very good impressions of the regal wave.

'I've got a sister-in-law who looks like the Queen Mum – just like her, same age. She's in a home.'

There is a sense of specially shared excitement. At 11.45 the police arrive. At 12.04 the carpet squad go into action, nailing a strip of red carpet – actually nailing it – into the tarmac of the road. At 12.25 the doors of the Kings Arms opposite open, and the pub's congregation spill out on to the pavement.

When she does appear, it happens very quickly. Grocer Delaney presents his flowers and ginger mints. She shakes hands with Mr and Mrs Fogarty. She talks and smiles to some of the people standing by the door. Then suddenly she is back in her car, and the maroon Daimler whisks her silently away.

It does not seem very much to have waited so long for, but the crowd breaks up beaming, chattering happily, fulfilled. Philip Delaney is the centre of attention, glowing with the royal touch.

'What did she say to you, Philip? *What did you say to her?*'

There are half a dozen reporters, a local television crew even.

'Well, I thanked her for coming, and she thanked me for the flowers. She said she was delighted to be here. She said she would eat the mints on her way home in the car this evening. I told her it was eighteen years now that we had been meeting like this and that she should not feel that she had to go on keeping it up. But she wouldn't hear of it. She said she would not dream of stopping.

'"It's a tradition we've got going here, Mr Delaney," she said. "And traditions exist to be kept."'

ou have to phone two or three weeks ahead for an appointment with the Textile Department at the Victoria & Albert Museum. Then, on the day, you go downstairs, through back corridors, past packing cases and ceiling-high metal grilles that protect Etruscan vases and medieval manuscripts and goodness knows what other treasures, until you come to a locked door. There it lies inside on a table: 'State evening dress 1959. Norman Hartnell. Worn and donated by HM Queen Elizabeth the Queen Mother.'

It is laid out reverently, like a vestment on an altar, a holy garment – and a rare one. It is one of the great royal mysteries, what happens to old royal clothes, the question that the press office can never answer exactly, or tries to slide around with a joke. This cream and blue ballgown escaped, with its owner's consent, via an exhibition loan that became permanent. So here it lies in a dusty, archival kingdom of prints and tiles and wallhangings, entombed for eternity for the scrutiny of academics who will come along with their pencils and magnifying glasses and explain to us exactly what beauty might be.

The dress is not really beautiful, though, when laid out flat and empty like this on the slab. Deprived of its essential filling, it is actually rather sad: the satin which hangs limp, the dulled glass beads and brilliants, the old nylon netting that has gone quite stiff and grey. Is this the magic of the Winterhalter Queen? The royal press office is correct. Just as royal visits bestow a sort of benediction, so royal dresses belong in the surplice and chasuble category, precious coverings to be marvelled at and worshipped, if you care to – and then burnt.

Royal men have their uniforms, their gold braid, their epaulettes, their medals and spurs. Royal ladies have to work out a uniform of their own, and this is what Norman Hartnell and Queen Elizabeth did together. Her racing manager, Michael Oswald, was struck one day by the fact that, whenever he went out with the Queen Mother to look at horses, she always wore the same light blue or light green raincoat, and that she never seemed to get cold. Oswald himself would have to muffle up with several layers of covering on some occasions, and he assumed that her apparently unvarying costume was a witness to her hardiness – which, in part, it was.

What he did not know was that his employer is the owner of more than one light blue raincoat and more than one light green – several of each, in fact, with different linings that, between them, take care of every kind of temperature. Non-royal mortals who could afford more than half a dozen raincoats might try for some different cuts and patterns. She understands about uniform.

'She has adopted one style, and she sticks to it,' says Evelyn Elliott, the Hartnell vendeuse who has looked after the Queen Mother's clothes for more than twenty-five years. 'The art of dressing is to know what you look good in.'

She spends hours on her fittings – hours and hours and hours. She has friends, male on the whole, who have seen her in Scotland in her old tweeds and battered felt hats, and who will consequently tell you with perfect assurance, 'Of course, she's not really that interested in what she wears.' They have not seen the long succession of mornings and afternoons blocked off in her calendar for no other purpose than the trying on of clothes. She just loves it. 'Oh, how *lovely*!' 'I'm going to *thoroughly* enjoy wearing that!' 'Am I being *too* extravagant?'

The answer to this last question is almost certainly yes. She is a very good spender. There is a joke in the royal family that Coutts & Co. would have folded long ago without the interest on the Queen Mother's overdraft. The problem for a vendeuse is not to sell her dresses, but to restrain her from ordering more than the workshop can make up in the time. In the 1960s and '70s, when she was working a very full programme, she would get through forty or fifty of her daytime 'outfits' in silk or velvet, each with coat and hat, not to mention her tailored coats and suits – and then there was the evening wear. All of this was paid for in full and on time. Princess Marina used to send back her half dozen outfits to Hartnell at the end of every season, but the Queen Mother never asks for favours.

The vendeuse comes first with the sketches – something strikingly blue for presenting the shamrock to the Irish Guards on St Patrick's Day, something that will not clash with the Mounties' red coats on her regular June visit to Canada. (When royal ladies talk of these considerations they like to emphasize how very *practical* they have to be.) The fabric swatches are clipped to the designs, and they are all gone through carefully. 'Perhaps another time' is her way of saying no – occasionally. Then the workshops get stitching.

Three to four weeks later, the vendeuse is back, now accompanied by a dressmaker, a soft tailor, who has made the lightweight velvet and silk coats, and by a master tailor, who is in charge of proper wool coats and jackets. This visiting team of four is joined by Her Majesty's senior dresser and junior dresser – two ladies – plus whichever of her pages and footmen is involved in serving the party with refreshment. Then for a couple of hours the entire company whirls into a ballet of pins and snippings and tuckings and paddings – 'a little of *this*?' 'Perhaps some *mmmmm* here?', 'I am sure it will be a *great* joy when it is finished.'

And that is only the first fitting. There will be at least one more before the 'great joy' arrives to be unpacked and appreciated and then hung in one of the tall wardrobes on the Clarence House upper floor. They are all up there, bar the odd escapee in the Victoria & Albert and one or two other costume museums – almost everything she has worn for the past half century, shrouded in ghostly white covers, rail after rail, each dress with a label saying where it was worn, and when. Her wedding dress by Handley Seymour is up there, cosseted in tissue paper in a big striped cardboard box, and, of course, the triumph, the white wardrobe for Paris.

In 1963 Cecil Beaton published his book *Royal Portraits* containing pictures from his 1939 photo session, and he sent her a copy. 'The years telescope,' she wrote in thanks, 'and suddenly I remembered what I felt like when I wore those pre-war garden party clothes – all those years ago.'

n May she will be across the road, sniffing the exotic blooms at the Chelsea Flower Show, but today she has to deal with plainer foliage. It is 17 March 1987, St Patrick's Day, and Her Majesty is due at Chelsea Barracks to present the shamrock to the Irish Guards.

It is another of those 'old' traditions which is not quite as old as it seems. It is not even, in fact, as old as she is. The Lady Elizabeth Bowes Lyon had already been seven months in the world when Queen Alexandra first sent boxes of shamrock to the newly formed Irish Regiment of Foot Guards in March 1901. In those days Ireland was all British. The Irish Guards were fierce men from Limerick, Killarney and County Cork, and out on parade today at Chelsea Barracks there is still a fair sprinkling of those Irishmen from south of the border – the Republic – all tricked out in their bearskins and scarlet.

Does not that make for some security problems – Southern Irishmen in British uniforms? You never know what the IRA might not try.

'Oh, the lads are very sensible about it, you know' – this said looking round warily. 'They keep a low profile when they go home.'

It is interesting that the risk is perceived as being to the guardsmen, the six-foot-tall soldiers who are out on the parade ground currently stamping the tarmac to death – not to the little figure in blue who has come among them unprotected by anything much more than ostrich feathers and a handbag.

The blue has been chosen to match the cockades in all the guardsmen's bearskins – a good strong kingfisher hue. It is a day for strong colours: pipers in green with saffron kilts, officers in gold frogging, Chelsea pensioners in red with tricorn hats – and all the wives and loved ones of the regiment, who have turned out in their finery for an occasion that is happier than a few that they have gathered for.

Today is a treat, and the Queen Mother is there to help make it so. You cannot get too serious about grown men pinning greenery in their bonnets – or solemnly inflicting the same indignity on a harmless dog. Connor, the mascot of the Irish Guards, has just joined the regiment. An Irish Wolfhound, grey and shambling, he succeeds Cormac of Tara, a nonconformist spirit who is recorded on the company conduct sheet as being guilty of 'Conduct to the prejudice of good order and military discipline contrary to section 69 of the Dog Act 1955 in that he at Pirbright on 17 Mar 77 failed to eat the sweets offered to him by Her Majesty Queen Elizabeth the Queen Mother.' Punishment: restricted visits to the stud.

The wispy greenery is distributed to the rest of the regiment in shallow wicker correspondence trays – the logistics of the Irish Guards, it seems, operate on similar principles to those of Clarence House – and then Her Majesty withdraws to the reviewing stand.

'Irish Guardsmen!' comes the command, 'remove your headdress!'

Across the parade ground the bearskins are lifted, then steadied at shoulder height.

'Irish Guardsmen! Three cheers for Her Majesty Queen Elizabeth the Queen Mother!' And there ring out across the parade ground towards the reviewing stand three gruff, gallant bellows of such homage as would bring a catch in the throat to any normally sentimental English – or Irish – man. The bearskins rise and fall three times.

Connor leads the marchpast. The drums beat. The pipes skirl – and bringing up the rear are the old campaigners, led by their officers in bowler hats, a whole platoon of them marching along, umbrellas furled. The City must have ground to a halt this morning.

Afterwards these old soldiers line up for an inspection by Her Majesty, an inspection just as she made of them ten, fifteen, twenty years ago. Two are in wheelchairs. One is linked to his neighbour by a short, white, blindman's staff, which he holds low, surreptitiously, as if the stick were not really there. Their shoulders are back, their chests are out. Their eyes say that they are not really here today in London on this grey, chilly morning, but in that other, earlier time when life was simpler, braver, younger – and the small, blue-clad lady who is coming down the line, smiling, nodding, so obviously pleased and proud of every single one of them, confirms that what they dream and remember really is quite true.

am at her feet,' declared Noel Coward in 1965. 'She has infinite grace of mind, charm, humour and deep-down kindness, in addition to which she looks enchanting.' The Queen Mother had come to lunch with him at his Jamaica home – bullshots on the veranda, then curry served in coconut shells, the whole feast topped off by strawberries and rum cream pie. 'The houseboy – by his special request – wore white gloves and a white coat. It was all tremendous fun... and she left behind her five gibbering worshippers.'

Nearly twenty years later, in March 1984, Queen Elizabeth the Queen Mother was guest of honour at a memorial service for Noel Coward in Westminster Abbey. She unveiled a stone to him: 'Noel Coward, Playwright, Actor, Composer – "A Talent to Amuse".' Flowers were laid at the stone by Joyce Carey, Sir John Mills, Evelyn Laye and Dame Anna Neagle. The Queen Mother was looking splendid, dressed in purple velvet and dripping with diamonds – Alastair Forbes said she must have had a win at Kempton the day before. Sir John Gielgud read the Coward poem, 'When I Have Fears':

When I feel sad, as Keats felt sad,
That my life is so nearly done
It gives me comfort to dwell upon
Remembered friends who are dead and gone...

Penelope Keith gave the Toast from *Cavalcade*, the gothic arches of the Abbey echoed to the haunting strains of 'Someday I'll Find You' and 'I'll See You Again', and by the time the Ambrosian Singers, standing in front of the altar, had sung the last note of 'London Pride' there was not a dry eye in the house.

If the Queen Mother lives to be a hundred, she will qualify for a telegram from the Palace. Sustained by a diet of regular work and mass adoration, she shows every sign of achieving that milestone. She does not carry out quite so many engagements as she used to, but still, in 1986, she managed a very respectable 130. Lord Thurso, her friend and neighbour up near the Castle of Mey in the tip of Caithness, wanted to invite her to a Highland ball, and arranged a special parlour to which she could withdraw whenever she felt like a rest. By one o'clock in the morning most of the other people at the party had come in for a minute or so, but the Guest of Honour was still out in action on the dance floor.

She has the knack of transmitting this energy to others. A not too distant evening at Royal Lodge, her home in Windsor Great Park, saw the venerable Lord Chancellor, Lord Hailsham (b.1907), throw aside his sticks to execute a respectably nimble Welsh jig – for a minute or so at least.

The transmission of feelings is her particular line of business. She radiates warmth and affection far beyond the capacity of one human being to generate, and that is because like all stars, she is a brilliant reflector. 'It is quite frightening sometimes,' says one of her ladies-in-waiting, 'to see the adoration in people's faces as she draws near. You can almost fell the love coming off them.'

The world perceives the British as an unemotional lot, and the world is not entirely wrong. But this nation which can have such sad difficulty, both communally and individually, in articulating its own feelings, seems to have no inhibitions whatever when it comes to expressing its love for a member of the royal family like Queen Elizabeth the Queen Mother. The more energetic do it by going out in the streets to wait and wave and cheer. The vast majority do it by reading the newspapers or, increasingly, by sitting at home in front of the television and feeling better after watching a royal programme – or so the ratings would seem to indicate – than they do at the end of the average soap opera. Either way, the emotions generated are predominantly matters of affection, pride and love, and these are healthy feelings to flush through any bloodstream.

Looking back, it all seems so obvious, so pre-ordained. But she has not reached the pinnacle of affection she now enjoys by luck, by deception or by anything other than her own good judgement. One of her horse-breeding friends describes her as an 'out-cross' – a term breeders use for fresh blood which is brought in to ginger up an established line of stock. The process is risky, but when it works, it can liven things up immeasurably. In her case, the effect has been almost entirely positive. The British royal family as it now stands – domestic, committed and so deft at public relations – is her creation as much as anyone else's. She has been a supportive wife to one sovereign and a creative mother to another. She has been a personality in her own right, twinkling and entrancing and radiating all the good will that a queen is supposed to radiate. In times of national difficulty she has been the very embodiment of courage and duty and grace and steadfastness – and she has managed to achieve all this because courageous, dutiful, graceful and steadfast turn out to be pretty good ways of describing what she is.

ACKNOWLEDGEMENTS

It must be because Queen Elizabeth the Queen Mother is such a prompt letterwriter herself that replies from any member of her staff seem to arrive invariably by return post, and quite often by telephone as well. In this, as in so many other respects, Clarence House sets an example which other royal households and departments might imitate with profit. This nimbleness has greatly aided the efficient – and, I hope, accurate – compilation of this book, and I am most grateful to Sir Martin Gilliat, the Queen Mother's Private Secretary, for his courtesy, helpfulness and attention to detail.

A number of people who are close to the Queen Mother spoke to me off the record. I am grateful to them, and also to Sir Harold Acton, Sir Alastair Aird, Lady Elizabeth Anson, Michael Barratt, David Cannadine, Nicholas Coleridge, Major Rags Courage, Valerie Cumming and the Museum of London, Philip Delaney, Frances Dimond and the Royal Archives at Windsor, the Earl of Drogheda, William and Nina Drummond, Evelyn Elliott, Sir Edward Ford, the Marquise de Ganay, Tim and Eileen Graham, Patricia, Viscountess Hambleden, Alan Hamilton, Major Tom Harvey, Nicholas Haslam, Kathy Henderson and the Humanities Research Center, Austin, Texas, Anthony Holden, Eileen Hose, The Hon. Elizabeth Lady Johnston, Ludovic Kennedy, Professor Sir Edmund Leach, Terry Lee, the London Library, the Countess of Longford, Valerie Mendes and the Victoria & Albert Museum, Sir Oliver Millar, Captain George Mitchison and Norman Hartnell Ltd, Rodney Moore, Sheridan Morley, Ann Morrow, Penelope Mortimer, John Mosnicka, Ann Paul, John Pearson, Michael and Lady Angela Oswald, Joy Quested-Nowell, Lady Jean Rankin, Dr Aileen Ribeiro, Kenneth Rose, Sir Geoffrey Shakerley, Michael Shea, Wing Commander Bill Simpson, the Earl of Snowdon, Dr Wayne Swift, Edda Tasiemka and the Hans Tasiemka Archive, Christopher Warwick, James Whittaker, Richard Young and Philip Ziegler.

Hugo Vickers has been particularly generous with his time and expertise. The accuracy of the text, particularly in the area of royal jewellery, owes much to the keen eye, knowledge and advice of Gerald Grant. Sara Driver worked indefatigably to secure the fresh and original pictures which make up two-thirds of the book. I am grateful to Bob Hook for undertaking the design with such grace and professionalism, and to Christine Marshall who typed, researched, rented cars, got train tickets and made so many things easy.

Michael Shaw believed in the idea when others, surprisingly, did not. David Driver helped set the original style. Bill Phillips and Gail Rebuck have been wise and exemplary editors. Mort Janklow and Ann Sibbald have been supportive from afar.

Because I was writing my family saw far too little of me over Easter. Still, the younger members got a holiday out of it, and to Sandi, my wife, who stayed behind to help and to sharpen the cutting edge of the creative process, my gratitude, as ever, goes beyond words.

Robert Lacey, May, 1987.